W9-AVB-165

LIBERATING PASSION

HOW THE WORLD'S BEST GLOBAL LEADERS PRODUCE WINNING RESULTS

LIBERATING PASSION

HOW THE WORLD'S BEST GLOBAL LEADERS PRODUCE WINNING RESULTS

Omar Khan
with
Paul B. Brown

WILEY
John Wiley & Sons (Asia) Pte. Ltd.

Copyright © 2008 by Omar Khan
Published in 2008 by John Wiley & Sons (Asia) Pte. Ltd.
2 Clementi Loop, #02-01, Singapore 129809

All rights reserved.

No part of this publication may be reproduced, stored in a retrieval system or transmitted in any form or by any means, electronic, mechanical, photocopying, recording, scanning or otherwise, except as expressly permitted by law, without either the prior written permission of the Publisher, or authorization through payment of the appropriate photocopy fee to the Copyright Clearance Center. Requests for permission should be addressed to the Publisher, John Wiley & Sons (Asia) Pte. Ltd., 2 Clementi Loop, #02-01, Singapore 129809, tel: 65-64632400, fax: 65-64646912, e-mail: enquiry@wiley.com.sg.

This publication is designed to provide accurate and authoritative information in regard to the subject matter covered. It is sold with the understanding that the publisher is not engaged in rendering professional services. If professional advice or other expert assistance is required, the services of a competent professional person should be sought.

Other Wiley Editorial Offices

John Wiley & Sons, 111 River Street, Hoboken, NJ 07030, USA

John Wiley & Sons, The Atrium Southern Gate, Chichester P019 8SQ, England

John Wiley & Sons (Canada), Ltd., 5353 Dundas Street West, Suite 400, Toronto, Ontario M9B 6H8, Canada

John Wiley & Sons Australia Ltd., 42 McDougall Street, Milton, Queensland 4064, Australia

Wiley-VCH, Boschstrasse 12, D-69469 Weinheim, Germany

Library of Congress Cataloging-in-Publication Data

ISBN   978-0-470-82313-2

Typeset in 11/13 point, Minister Light by C&M Digitals (P) Ltd.
Printed in Singapore by Saik Wah Press Pte. Ltd.
10   9   8   7   6   5   4   3   2   1

CONTENTS

DEDICATION

To my wife Leslie—my greatest Passion Liberator

ACKNOWLEDGMENTS

This book is possible because of the extraordinary stimuli I (Omar Khan) have received from so many exceptional and generous sources. Space allows me to highlight only a few.

On the most personal of fronts, my father has been since my childhood, an untiring stimulus in the realm of people, ideas, causes and effects of small and large-scale change, and how human beings have to institutionalize progress. As an ambassador, author and cultural bridge-builder this has been my father's avocation and passion.

My mother has modeled resilience, deep composure, tough love, compassion, and high degrees of social and emotional intelligence so that they became behavioral templates for me to seek to emulate and model far before I knew consciously what they were.

I owe an incalculable debt to Tom Peters. It is true Peter Drucker gave us the wherewithal to understand the knowledge worker, and almost founded management as a true practice that involves people and their interactions. But to me it is Tom Peters who not only vivified management, but humanized it, and brought human passions, energy, imagination and relationships to the core of business excellence. Tom continues to live and exemplify that message magnificently and incomparably to this day. I can only salute his spirit, intelligence and soul. It has been a pleasure to learn from him and to interact with him.

The enduring impact of the work of M. Scott Peck, best-selling author of *The Road Less Traveled* (among many other path-breaking books) on me was nothing short of transformational. Scotty taught me that relationships are intellectually demanding that they aren't "fluff," that they are the very foundation of creating true progress in society and in organizations. The work on community-building with his Foundation for Community

Encouragement (FCE), and my very intimate friendship and work with Scotty in the last several years of his life provided me with a fundamental new paradigm of how we can allow for personal authenticity and loving honesty as a way of moving collaboration and necessary results forward.

From my time working with the Strategic Coach, I have gained immensely from Dan Sullivan's entrepreneurial genius, the insights into creating and packaging value, and the capacity to convert both into powerful and practical tools. Dan has created a 21st century organization and showed me how to create an ever larger future that amplifies personal strengths as well as personal satisfaction. Underlying his work, is a great respect for human dynamics, and he provides tools to create exceptional conversations and interactions with colleagues, partners, customers and family.

Thanks go to maestro Benjamin Zander, conductor of the Boston Philharmonic and life enthusiast par excellence for being such a marvelous conduit for possibility. I acknowledge with appreciative enthusiasm the work of Ben and his wife Roz Zander in having rekindled my love affair with the concept of "possibility" as an antidote for the downward spiral discourse that otherwise threatens to dominate the business world.

Abundant thanks go to the team at Wiley in Singapore for believing in this project and for guiding it to completion.

More than anyone or anything, I have to thank my wife Leslie, who is my foil in all such projects, my life and business partner, my conscience-keeper, my feedback loop, my greatest friend, a source of beauty and nurturing, and my indefatigable cheerleader...truly she makes it all possible for me. I am both humbled and grateful by how completely I feel loved and supported by her.

CHAPTER 1

HOW THE WORLD'S BEST GLOBAL LEADERS PRODUCE WINNING RESULTS

The Missing Link

There is a missing link in all our talk about leadership.

We read about operational disciplines, execution, innovation, developing teams, situational leadership, recognizing and growing talent, leadership temptations, aptitudes and habits. But there is a wick running through the practice of leadership that needs far more explicit recognition and attention.

This missing link is the source of leadership energy, adaptation and perseverance.

It's passion.

Oh, we allude to it, tap dance around it, but no one has really nailed the connection yet.

We've Come Close

It seems a few years back, everyone in the management and leadership worlds discovered "passion." One of our favorite quotes comes from one of our clients who encapsulated the "discovery" this way: "Profits are the passion and talent of our team focused on the bottom-line."

Note, passion here is the kindling for talent—it is the great enabler, the open sesame.

Charles Handy, the eminent British management guru, opined that passion IS the answer. If you know the way forward, passion will amplify your energy, your commitment, your imagination. If you don't know how to proceed, it is passion that will drive you to find a way—to consult others, to prototype, to take risks, to be relentless in constructive ways.

Chief executive officers (CEOs) tout passion no less than management gurus do. Troll through the utterances or writings of Herbert Kelleher (Southwest), Jack Welch (formerly General Electric (GE)), Jeffrey Immelt (GE), James McNerney (formerly 3M now Boeing), Anita Roddick (Body Shop), Howard Schultz (Starbucks), Richard Branson (Virgin), Allan Leighton (U.K.'s Royal Mail), Lars Kolind (formerly Oticon), Carlos Ghosn (Nissan/Renault), and you'll find passion lurking never very far away.

Passion is the leadership software extraordinaire, they all say in one form or another. It lets us know our people have the energy and inner commitment necessary to translate potential into results.

We can only be grateful that such a critical human endowment has finally earned its justifiable pride of place, and that we finally recognize that passion is a key ingredient in success. However it is less encouraging how confused we are about what this all might entail in everyday action.

In fact, many people aren't exactly clear on how to even define the word.

There are many possible definitions of passion. But we are going to use it to mean the *voluntary will to engage completely; the inner energy, drive AND desire to deliver, to achieve, and to win.*

Article after article, speech after speech, seems to suggest that we have to somehow *build* passion; that we have to inculcate it in others. This is a mistake. The fact is the presence of passion is natural in all kinds of settings. *Its absence is what is profoundly unnatural.*

When children are born, they don't have a passion deficit. No mother wails for sympathy because her child isn't passionate enough about being alive. They yearn for a tranquilizer for the child perhaps, but not a stimulant.

Passion is natural when we do virtually anything—from playing touch football, to a game of cards with friends, to having conversations about politics or favorite movies.

No one needs a seminar about how to be passionate about a meal at a favorite restaurant or when listening to a beloved CD. Passion is abundant in so many places, except sadly at work.

This is not inevitable, this is by unfortunate design. For example, a major financial services company we've worked with is restructuring in order to be able to make key decisions globally and regionally, rather than at each local operation. This change is meant to be more "efficient." However, a global and regional bureaucracy with no idea of local market needs and expectations, and a bureaucracy glacially slow in response to requests from local offices, only succeed in killing the passion of their teams.

The local teams watch competitors swoop in with quick market initiatives, as they experience only immobilizing frustration and scant benefit from the new structure. Whenever the "game-changing" new structure is touted in company forums, it elicits cynical sneers and rolling eyes, rather than enthusiasm from their most capable local managers. Senior management ascribes the sneers to resistance to change. They don't realize that the inept functioning of the structure of their new organization is the real culprit.

So the real problem is not how you build passion. The real problem is to understand how we *kill* it. Companies have become exceptional *passion killers*. And that is painfully ironic.

Passionate people are hired in most leading companies (that's part of what gets them hired). Within three months, the passion has often been sucked out of them. Companies are "passion castrators" in so many ways.

Let's go through a few examples of how this happens:

- We often don't induct people properly. People don't understand their own roles; the goals of the company; the culture they are to participate in; how to legitimately win and forge forward in this new arena. Left adrift, they either become tentative, or get good at equivocation and diplomacy. None of this tends to stir our latent passion.

- We lack mentors. Without a mentor and/or coach, people try to apply what worked in their last position and often don't gain new skills, aptitudes or different ways of thinking. If they manage to produce results, it is often by compensating for what they *haven't* developed. They may get the job done but often dysfunctionally and often in a way that is excessively idiosyncratic. So let's say they haven't really evolved the ability to really listen with curiosity. But they may nevertheless be gifted at recovering and changing direction fast. Had they explored the situation openly with veteran front-liners, they may have found a more proactive and therefore less wasteful response. As a result when they move on, very little is left in their wake that can be taken forward, collective learning has been stunted rather than being institutionalized, and a vacuum is often what is left rather than a living culture. If these unmentored and under-coached managers continue their progress in the company, you can have very senior leaders bereft of elementary management skills or leadership abilities. Though they may have cultivated a knack for producing some results one way or another, the opportunity cost, the human debris, and the collective unfulfilled potential along the way can be devastating.

- Often there is scant feedback given until a formal review looms. Feedback when it is given tends to be negative. So people only learn what they aren't doing well. Not surprisingly, they try to duck feedback, since it is associated with negative reinforcement.

The last point above is particularly tragic. Feedback has to be a way of life. How else can we can get a read-out of how we are doing. How else can we enhance our abilities and ourselves?

But effective feedback has to be anchored in credibility. How can we earn the right for our perspective to be seen as credible as well as constructive, unless we truly understand the other person? We can compel *attention* through our hierarchical status, but we can't "command" credibility.

The primary way that credibility with our team is achieved is through a combination of consistent real-time appreciation *and* challenge. Only when both occur, do we trust either. Passion dies from insincere praise yes, but also from blinkered put downs.

Passion is also siphoned off when companies attack symptoms rather than root causes. A client we've worked with is keen to reduce costs. Their automatic reflex has been to ask executives to limit travel and all nonessential expenditure.

As a result, this globally networked company is discouraging leaders from traveling to see their customers, or from having key interactions with colleagues they need to confer with if an aligned global strategy is to be rolled out.

However, multiple meetings mandated by the CEO and the global board, often just to hear PowerPoint presentations, bringing together the top leaders from around the world, continue uninhibited. These internal exchanges are mere formalities, since all these presentations have been vetted by senior leaders en route to being ready for presentation.

Of course it is a waste of hundreds of thousands of dollars to get 40 of the company's top leaders to a central resort location to see something that could have been handled by email or a video conference. But you have to ask yourself how many millions of dollars more the company is pouring down the drain, by taking these senior executives away from their markets, away from their customers, and putting in largely pro forma time, and having them go home bored and dispirited when they find that no "real" issues have been tabled, no real conflicts faced and transcended, and no real relationships forged or meaningfully deepened?

Unfortunately, there are endless similar examples of how we manage to muffle, diminish and outright kill passion.

Are there antidotes? Yes, there are, and they go to attacking and eliminating the underlying malaise that runs through all such examples.

One such underlying problem is the quality and authenticity (or lack thereof) of relationships among the leaders of the business and in fact throughout the organization.

Leadership is fundamentally about how we relate to others, how we engage, mobilize, focus and ignite each other—or fail to.

Our impact on each other, and the authenticity, imagination and commitment with which we engage is a fundamental source of passion.

So as we proceed together in this adventure of rescuing and unleashing passion, we'll first take a deeper look at the passion problem and gain an understanding of how this problem arises. (Chapter 2) Presumably we don't set out to leech passion away from each other. Why then is killing passion almost universal as a management practice? We will answer that question here.

We'll then explore how success comes from successful relationships, and see how relationship pathologies are at the root of virtually every corporate dysfunction. (Chapter 3) These inauthentic and often corrosive relationships are clearly a significant component in the destruction of passionate engagement. We'll gain an insight into how to restore relationships to their rightful role as the prime architects of a leadership culture.

In the next section, we will look at the antidotes. Chapters 4–12 will explore at length the nine passion liberators. Each of these actually turns a different tumbler in our heads, hearts and spirits. By understanding each of these passion liberators, we'll also understand the most chronic, destructive and repetitive passion killers so we can avoid them and empower their alternatives.

In the final section, we'll take a look at arguably the most critical aspect of all this. Having understood both the magnitude of this problem, and the solution, the question is how can we generate a purposeful and pragmatic game plan to convert the passion liberators into our organization's daily leadership habits?

The answer to that question can be found in chapters 13 and 14.

Can we truly deliver a high passion, high performance work culture? Yes! And we'll see precisely how, drawing, in part, from the actual experience of those who have.

Overall, we have to eliminate the division between who we are and what we do. We have to learn to convert leadership from a set of grand intentions into a wonderful way to engage and evoke the best in each other. We have to stop "educating" passion out of people.

Albert Einstein famously warned us, "Our problems will not be solved by the same level of thinking that gave rise to the problems in the first place."

That's absolutely correct! And they won't be solved by the same lack of emotional maturity or the same absence of relationship authenticity or the same failure of personal courage to grow that gave rise to these problems either.

Let's liberate our latent passion and that of our teams! There is no better source of, or report card for, organizational and personal excellence.

CHAPTER 2

THE GREAT PASSION HEIST

We've already argued that passion is a natural endowment. We are born with it in abundance. It gushes from us when we're young, and in situations where we are comfortable and happy (time with friends, hobbies, challenges we care about, frolic with loved ones). At those times, no secret recipes, incantations or inducements are required.

It is also clear, that when we operate from passion, we are enlivened; our creativity is heightened, we think more clearly. And the effect on others is profound. We are a pleasure to deal with; we encourage and enthuse others far more.

In short, we are more productive, more imaginative, and are also more likely to have the energy for expressing real compassion and for taking an extra step to serve or to support others.

Given all this, you would naturally think that companies would not only seek to hire passionate people, but would do everything in their power to preserve this passion, to stoke it, to nurture and stimulate it, to honor those leaders who seem to evoke it in others and thereby further the ability and reach of their teams.

You would think so. But you would be tragically wrong.

The statistics on disengagement of people in workplaces is horrifying. The Gallup organization estimates that as many as seven out of 10 workers are "disengaged" and the concomitant loss of productivity, quality, effectiveness, and profitability are immeasurable. We say "immeasurable" because it is hard to measure a negative. It is hard to even begin to quantify so encompassing an opportunity cost.

Why and how does this problem arise? With everyone acknowledging the power of passion, with the most admired companies from Body Shop to Virgin to Southwest to Toyota, showcasing zealous, animated employee-advocates; why and how do companies manage to so consistently be passion extinguishers?

The answer boils down to a fundamental dividing line between almost all human activities and therefore all corporate initiatives.

We can divide virtually all human activity into the "technical" and the "growth-based." Consider parenting. The "technical" side of parenting involves making sure children have clothing, are fed, have a decent home environment, get schooling, learn some basic discipline and life habits. We can call this the "infrastructure" of parenting.

While we would have to concede this is adequate for raising a child, it certainly doesn't paint a portrait likely to melt many hearts or touch many spirits. Listed as above, the activities seem like a straightforward, or even, drab set of duties. It is the parenting equivalent of painting by the numbers: efficient, but not very meaningful.

The growth-based side of parenting conceives of the act as fostering both parent and child. The parent learns by stilling their ego, by making room for the needs of another, by dedicating themselves to the fulfillment and actualization of another life, ideally in intimate collaboration with a life partner. The child is stimulated by being unconditionally cared for, and yet loved enough to also be confronted, and challenged, and exposed to new and invigorating experiences. The child's esteem is fostered because being supported and loved gives him or her the confidence to experiment, to adventure, to learn, to fail, to grow and to have the courage to take responsibility. Hopefully, being loved and supported also gives the child a sense of gratitude and the capacity to in turn support, care for and stand by others.

Seen in this way, the passage from birth to adulthood is the hero's journey that has been eulogized and mythologized throughout literature. Examples abound from knight quests in earlier lore, to tales of enlightenment and awakening in spiritual traditions, or even more modern sagas of exploration and redemption like Lord of the Rings or even Star Wars. It is a grand quest demanding our greatest insight, resilience, courage and wisdom. For this undertaking, passion is almost always an abundant and renewable resource.

Now, keeping in mind the enormous difference between these two vantage points (the technical and the growth-based) let's return to corporate life. Let's take a number of seminal examples: corporate strategy, winning with customers, and developing human resources, and examine how this dividing line between technical and growth-based provides us a penetrating explanation for the diminishing of otherwise natural passion.

Corporate Strategy

As is clear from the discussion on parenting, the "technical" is inevitably the easiest default route to take. It requires mustering far less energy, vitality, and personal courage than the growth-based alternative which demands personal adaptation and evolution.

Let's look at what happens when companies dive into the "technicalities" of corporate strategy and forget that at least 50% of strategy involves communicating, enrolling, engaging and executing—all things that clearly are growth-based. If those growth-based activities are not incorporated, strategy too often becomes a tedious "planning" exercise and not a passionate envisioning, challenging, prioritizing, intelligence-tapping excursion that leads to what strategy really should be: our best bet on how to win in key markets and influence the industry by dramatic differentiation.

"Strategy" often ends up becoming a bureaucratic nightmare rather than a compass and a launch-pad when teams are subjected to a cycle of iterative improvement planning sessions (last year plus 10%); and/or to passively imbibe a huge number of top-down initiatives (many of which will never see the light of day as the world changes around us); and are assigned to numerous task forces (many of which will fizzle out as enthusiasm wanes and quarterly numbers have to be delivered).

But it does not have to be this way. A.G. Lafley of Procter & Gamble (P&G) for example holds "bare knuckle" (hard-hitting exchanges where candor trumps politeness) strategy sessions in P&G about "where will we play" and "how will we win," where the best ideas throughout the organization are reviewed and debated. Decisions, expectations and actions that flow from these exchanges are tracked, and the whole organization is held accountable for what is agreed to. Conducted this way, strategy becomes an exhilarating cutting-edge experience.

Herb Kelleher of Southwest famously intoned: "We have a strategic plan, it's called doing things." Provocative, if a bit too glib, his comments outline a far better approach than the one that comes out of the "technicalities" school. I'd reword Kelleher's comment slightly to say, "Pick your best positioning and then do things, gather fast feedback, re-calibrate, and do some more things." In other words, find a value dimension where you feel you can have strategic advantage and thereafter, treat strategy as an emergent process—where antennae have to be up, listening posts and relay stations have to be set up (throughout the organization, the market, and within our top customers as well), and fast coordinated response has to be a high art. Passion then will be on successful display.

Winning with Customers

The grand old man of management, Peter Drucker, once reminded us that the purpose of a business is to create a customer. Indeed. But thereafter, the purpose has to be to help that customer succeed and win through us.

When winning the customer, helping the customer win, and thereby winning with the customer becomes "technical," we start proliferating databases, CRM tools, we launch campaigns, promotions, and spend undue amounts of energy on the glitziest ad campaigns. We set up customer hotlines (though finding a live human on one of these today requires the most extreme acrobatics), websites, and more.

On the other hand, the growth-based approach means to bring the customer to the very core of our business, our processes, our systems, our decisions, our people, our training, our leadership, all of it.

By itself, how excited will anyone be by the fact that a company owns a website? Not very. But even a website can be growth-based in the sense of being responsive to real human desires and preferences and seek to adapt accordingly. In this vein, compare most drab websites with the remarkably user-friendly, consummately interactive Amazon.com, which actually evolves, based on what a customer enters during each visit. Amazon's obsession with convenience, customization and ordering satisfaction literally seeps out of the website.

This kind of attempt at trying to get close to the customer should be a venerable practice rather than a passing novelty.

During Motorola's heyday, then CEO Robert Galvin spent time on the customer complaint lines. Bob Townsend did the same when he headed up Avis. Why? Because it gave them unfiltered information. But this was also important because it broadcast the primacy of the customer in the most visceral way possible. More recently, this same primacy is demonstrated by initiatives like "At the Customer for the Customer" (ACFC) at GE, which is about helping customers solve the problems *they* are facing, strategizing with them, sending members of GE's teams to customers' sites—supporting customers on issues that matter (even on products or services that are unrelated) on the belief that successful customers are better customers.

So getting out of our functional silos, and into the mind and heart and spirit of our customer or consumer, requires adaptation and growth. A collection of their phone numbers and buying preferences doesn't translate into our understanding them or help us understand them in a way that influences our decisions, products and services.

For that, we need to think about our customers differently. We need to stop thinking about them only as dollar signs and start thinking of them as people whose lives and priorities we have to understand so we can really help (and thereby attract more business naturally). If we take this approach, not only will we improve our customers' lives, but also our own excitement for and satisfaction with what we do every day.

Employees can't be passionate about hotlines. They can and will be passionate when they see that customers literally "love" to do business with us, that our hotline is a delight, that consumers are "lit up" with excitement at using our product or service—when, as it has been said, we create as much of a "cause" as a "business."

This doesn't just mean our organizations need to do socially valuable things, important though that can be. It means having a messianic devotion to the success, satisfaction, and positive surprise we offer those who ultimately pay us to be in existence.

The FedEx "absolutely, positively has to be there the next day" promise is a credo of this type. The Four Seasons Hotels wanting you to feel "homesick for a hotel" is a living dedication. No amount of forms, or databases, or call infrastructure, will stir the latent abilities and commitment of our people, much less our customers, in this way. A passionate purpose calls forth passionate action.

Human Resources

As a global consultant Omar has spent a career largely trying to duck human resource (HR) people. As someone who primarily helps senior leaders and leadership teams get the most from each other and their strategies, in terms of performance and profits by emotionally engaging them, it may seem odd that HR managers aren't his company's most natural allies.

Sensei International has of course had the pleasure of partnering with a few exceptional ones. But they have largely been rare exceptions. The reason is that "human resources" (horrible term) or "talent management" or whatever the *appellation-de-jour*, have, for the most part, become administrative hacks, divorced from performance, or leadership, or culture. And so, far from championing the people and talent perspective, they become administrative inquisitors checking for "compliance" against various programs or standards that are rarely, if ever, checked to see if they make a true difference.

Here again, the reason is that the "technical" aspects of managing the human factor in organizations come so much easier, and require so much less energy, insight and personal effort.

HR departments are these days fond of asserting that they have achieved "best in class" status. This pompous bit of self-congratulation simply means that their organization has the processes and systems in line with what is the currently accepted best thinking in the field.

Of course, it is important that there are job descriptions and classifications, that there is a hiring and firing policy, that there be induction, performance management, career management and more. But the presence of a process tells us nothing about the commitment or integrity or impact with which it is wielded.

Take performance management reviews. Most are largely a waste of time, despite all the forms being filled in, an interview taking place, and everything being signed off by both appraiser and appraisee. Why? Because a performance review assumes there has been active coaching throughout the year. The *ne plus ultra* of such reviews should be that nothing shared in the formal review can be a surprise. In other words, if it merits time and attention in the annual review, then it was important enough for real-time feedback and active coaching when the person could actually do something about it.

A real commitment to the person's development, being his talent scout, mentor, and if he plays the game well, his advocate and public relations (PR) agent if necessary, is a growth-based leadership agreement that will drive the person forward with gusto to deliver on the future development and delivery targets agreed upon.

Otherwise, the exercise is not developmental. It is simply to secure nominal acquiescence in how to describe the current status quo, and the performance appraisal is useful for little more than to dispense bonus and debate increments. "Performance" then becomes a rather blatant angling for popularity with the boss/appraiser and the "review" becomes a matter of managing appearances.

Take the all-important job of filling a leadership pipeline. Technically oriented HR people say there is a vacancy in a critical high-profile job and then scavenge around looking for a feasible replacement among those who are deemed to have "potential." Often, those with potential haven't been proactively given the assignments and development opportunities that will draw out that potential. So we may get someone very talented but not yet ready. Then, and almost worse, the HR folk look for the most currently experienced, if often uninspired "ready" replacement—even though in sober moments these candidates would never have been considered for this magnitude of role. But by default, they are who we have.

Compare this with a growth-based approach like that pioneered by GE and now increasingly evident at companies like Microsoft where talent reviews are every bit as important as budget reviews. There an absolutely critical part of a key annual meeting involves a look at talent bench strength, a vigorous look at the development needs and potential of leaders at various key levels of the organization, and a committed plan with transparent accountability to hone and evoke what each of them can best deliver. And this is passionately debated and ultimately agreed to by the CEO, all senior leaders, along with the talent/ HR professionals of the organization.

In such companies, HR sizzles, and people are passionate because their leaders, and their company are also passionate about them.

Passion Killers

When we take a step back, we can see why passion killers abound and are so devastatingly omnipresent. In passion-killing events every undertaking is trivialized into a set of technical actions, formats, formulae and injunctions. Vitality, real relevance and appeal are leeched.

We are not in a crusade against the "technical" aspects of growth. These are critically needed. They are just not sufficient for summoning human capability, energy and imagination. For example, we all need floors and walls and doors for a dwelling. But they give you a house at best. A home is still something you have to create.

And so, virtually every endeavor has a dimension that speaks to its highest transformational potential. This invariably demands our own evolution, our own growth, the adaptation of our behaviors and skills, and sometimes a retooling of how we think and respond. This is a call to re-invention.

Leadership is essentially an act of ongoing re-invention. And people engaged in re-invention—even when it is difficult or sometimes precisely because it is challenging in a way that matters—are alive with passion, with what has been poetically called *élan vital*, the life force.

Now, one practical way forward is to assemble any team that has to produce a result together and get them to catalogue the "passion killers" they actually experience.

If you go this route, your lists will often include examples like boring endless meetings; lengthy emails rather than personal contact; lack of consumer insight driving decisions; hypercritical evaluation of ideas; inadequate positive recognition; lack of coaching; interdepartmental conflict; and so on.

These are big issues, big challenges, and big opportunities. (More on that in a minute.)

If your own list of passion killers has more modest problems—like eliminating meeting A, or revising form B, or resolving one key conflict between two individuals, or committing to send everyone on a team-building session, go for it! Eliminate all the low-hanging passion killers for sure. Be as decisive, visible, collective and dramatic as possible. You will create enormous goodwill and receive a veritable gusher of appreciation.

However, if the needs are more expansive, more woven into the very fabric of life in your organization—as we saw with the first list—then you will need a more fundamental understanding of what is arguably the pre-eminent passion killer, the one Gordian Knot that has to be cut before proposed remedies can have any sustained success.

It is only by grappling with this most fundamental of barriers that we can get to the passion liberators this book is really about. These passion liberators are interactions, behaviors and tools that can take us forward to the vision and culture we truly want. They *energize our potential*—which is ultimately what passion and so much of leadership are all about.

Let's therefore examine and find how to effectively grapple with this radical (coming from the Latin *radix*, root) passion killer. That is what we turn to next.

CHAPTER 3

COMMUNICATING AS A LAST RESORT...

If you look at most of our problems, both big and small, one thing is glaringly evident. Most of them are fundamentally problems of communication. And that is true whether we are talking about wrecked personal relationships, or wars. Our planet is littered with the wreckage of failed communication.

There is also currently a fad in certain foreign policy circles to say we should only communicate with those who agree with us, or as a reward for good behavior. The implication seems to be that to communicate with a transgressor is to somehow, tacitly, at least, to condone their transgressions.

This is particularly ironic since the very purpose of foreign policy, at least in large part, is to reduce tensions *through communication* using a judicious mixture of carrots and sticks; by mapping out likely scenarios; by balancing interests and by drawing on other allies who have influence. This is what we used to call diplomacy.

Closer to home, America's founding fathers expected there to be divisive interests, polarization, and competing needs in the country they created. They prepared for that to be worked out constructively through a system of checks and balances, of three theoretically co-equal branches of government. This structure was designed to *mandate communication* for that is the only way a three-way deadlock would potentially be averted.

But of late we see such theory lagging far behind practice in national politics, as well as in international relations, even in commercial life evidenced in the ongoing proliferation of lawsuits. Lawyers rather than being a medium of communication have become a medium for almost entrenched contention.

It seems clear that we humans will "consider" communicating and building relationships only as a last resort. And so we are led quite naturally to the canopy passion killer we mentioned earlier. This canopy passion killer is the lack of quality and authenticity in the relationships among the leaders of the business and in fact throughout the organization. Let us demonstrate why we make this claim.

If you fantasized a company in which personal maturity and the quality and integrity of relationships *weren't* the fulcrum, we'd have a wonderfully Panglossian (Pangloss was a rose-tinted optimist in Voltaire's classic *Candide)* picture, rather than the Prufrockian (the despondent lovelorn lamenter in T.S. Eliot's monumental poem) reality that actually prevails.

Let's Pretend

Imagine a company that has a product or service of value to the marketplace. They've found a way to produce and/or deliver it in a cost-effective and reasonably compelling way. The product or service is distinctive enough and the company has managed to communicate that distinction competently enough that they have developed a brand identity. And we will assume that there has been enough success up until now to allow them to invest in top-drawer talent. As there is an upward trajectory, and decent press, good people even "want" to join.

Given the buzz, customers are eager to give the company a try, and investment capital isn't currently scarce. There are opportunities for expansion, for alliances, and more.

Now into this hypothetical we inject a talented CEO, one selected on merit. In a world in which maturity or relationship issues weren't primary deterrents, such a talented person, with an essentially viable enterprise, would likely proceed in the following manner:

He/she would gather a talented and diverse leadership team that was aligned in overall values. Such a leader would find out, through whatever means possible, his/her own natural aptitudes, and fortify areas which weren't natural strengths, with the abilities of others.

This leader would want a robust and vital leadership pipeline, with considerable energy going into mutual engagement, idea exchange, and learning flowing throughout the organization.

He/she would ensure the company set up listening posts at various customer epicenters and would ensure that the customers and the company innovated together, possibly even strategized together. "Customer success" would be an overarching metric for success in this company.

Improvement would be the order of the day. The past would be consulted for lessons, but challenged unromantically on a daily basis in order to continually raise the bar, to push for a larger and more prosperous future.

Humility and deep listening would be non-negotiables. A hunger for new ideas, a curiosity for everything that's happening out in the world, would be abundant among all leaders. These stimuli would be filtered back to the organization to inspire both innovation and decision-making via ongoing dialogue, actively consulted and frequently updated databases, meetings and forums, to inspire both innovation and decision-making.

Feedback would be venerated above all else, no matter from where. Members of the organization would go seeking it. It would be the "Holy Grail," whether coming from suppliers, or customers, or analysts, or thinkers, or poets, or sociologists, or anyone who interacts with us and our part of the world.

When the organization decided on courses of action, it would then be able to, on the basis of all of the above, have huge buy-in, move decisively, and execute powerfully.

Before proceeding much further, it must be clear that 97% of even "successful" enterprises do not resemble this portrait at all. In fact, the case we presented seems like a utopian fable at best, fevered myopia at worst.

But why? Why would this not flow naturally and inevitably from rational, talented people, wanting to maximize the current and future performance of their business in an increasingly interconnected and competitive world?

And the reason we come back to is that the barrier is not rationality, is not talent, is not ability, and is not perspicacity. It is our emotional maturity and the relationships between us and the key others in our organization that make or break this reality.

IBM Consulting's annual CEO survey identified one of the biggest fears of leaders as not having next-level leaders ready and able to lead the future. This is extraordinary if you think about it! Senior leaders who themselves determine, to some extent, the availability, quality and readiness of next-level leaders, identify not having enough of them as one of their biggest anxieties!

The most logical explanation is that THEY personally lack the energy and perhaps ability to enroll, develop, coach, catalyze and create the developmental relationships that would generate the leaders they are looking for.

Speaking of IBM, during the 1990s, in the pre-Gerstner era, Robert Heller in chronicling the misadventures of this period reports: "Where John Akers failed, in the eyes of the board, investors, and his successor, was in the wrong execution of the right strategy... Akers had plainly failed to achieve the true object of reinvention: to change, not the organization, but the behavior of those within... *None of the remedies had worked, because the reinventors couldn't reinvent the most crucial element of all: themselves.*"

In roughly 14 years of Sensei International's global work spanning the U.S., U.K., the Middle East, South Asia and East Asia, we've seen this show up again and again. The personality of the leaders literally seeps into both the architecture as well as the bloodstream of the organization. How focused is the organization, how disciplined, how open, how creative, how encouraging of diversity, how nimble—all depend on the psychodynamics of the key individuals *and the chemistry (or lack thereof) and friction between them.* And with the quality and integrity of these relationships, the passion killers are either routed, or else ooze out.

Here's Why This is So Hard

Passion killers remain in place, despite their evident destructive impact, because to confront them would require re-engineering fundamental attitudes and beliefs that show up most evidently in relationships. The passion killers either sprout in the first place due to poor relationships (for example being caused by inadequate consultation, collaboration or alignment) or else aren't challenged openly when in place because of the paltry relationships that prevail.

Some years ago an Hewlett-Packard (HP) safety leader, Bob Veazle, influenced by his experience with the "network of conversations" approach exemplified by the World Café methodology, launched a series of conversations about safety across various HP units.

The World Café works by setting up multiple rounds of conversations between diverse groups of people with each round of conversation building on the last. In each round, you dialogue with a different group of people. At each dialogue location, a host remains from the last conversation, who updates the new group as to what the conversation has been at that location. Each of the joining members inputs insights and points from their own last round of conversations. Then, collectively, they build on and extend from the distilled inputs that were shared. Multiple rounds occur, each time a different host remains, and the dialogue groups always shift. In short, World Café is a set of cross-pollinating, iterative conversations on a core topic.

Bob Veazle realized that a network of crucial conversations was an exciting and empowering paradigm by which to conceive of organizations and organizational communication. Accordingly, he envisaged boxes on the organizational chart as "webs of conversations." So instead of multiple rounds of dialogue in a conference room, he realized multiple dialogues between functions and leaders and locations could be set up—each of which drew upon and built on previous conclusions and interactions.

As these freer flowing conversations about safety supplanted more rigid safety programs that had been tried and had petered out, an amazing thing happened. Full-time safety leaders became "conversation hosts" and, whether they knew it or not, relationship-nurturers (because they were enabling vital conversations that bound people together—about possible life and death, injury and health, between those whose everyday behavior could make a decisive impact to each other). Injury and accident rates plummeted, hitting best in the world measures in certain key locations. Even years later, Bob reported, people in HP continued to refer to new challenges by saying "Why don't we tackle it like we did safety?" In other words, by having multiple conversations between people who can make a difference, by generating and passing on ideas and insights and experiences, almost like batons, from one community to another within the company—inviting each to add their own piece of experience to enrich the larger whole. "Handling it like safety" is a plea Carly Fiorina would have done well to tune into, as one of the authors knows personally from having spent some time with HP/Compaq in the Middle East during her reign.

Most interesting about the safety example is that in the aftermath of this effort, one of the sites, while still 50% improved over its original safety record, began to slide back. Their Puerto Rico site remained a world leader in terms of safety record continuously for years thereafter.

The difference it seems came down to Puerto Rico continuing to host their own internal safety conversations *as a way of life*. In the other locations, Bob Veazle's new approach was treated as a "program," and fissures developed as relationships and conversations weren't maintained.

What Needs to be Done

The moral from the HP example and a multitude of other similar examples is clear: *there is a level and quality of conversational and relational leadership required to sustain change and improvement until it becomes truly integrated*. Otherwise we have "breakthroughs" but they don't last. This new kind of leadership interaction does two things. Through wide-scale and ongoing engagement, it first liberates the passion to *create* a new way forward. *And* secondly, if maintained, it also stokes the passion to *sustain* the breakthrough once it takes place.

And this in turn suggests the link between personal maturity and relationships and the business results we are seeking.

Perhaps the greatest organizational opportunity we have is to foster the emotional maturity and resulting openness of leaders. Accompanying this are the necessary and far less rare rational apparatus of industry knowledge, the ability to think clearly about facts, and decision-making ability among others. We then become "fit" for relationships.

Relationships in turn are the alchemy we need for the base metal (our technical proficiency) to become gold (creative, adaptive achievement).

And when we create authentic, thriving relationships, we keep the most tenacious and pernicious passion killers from taking root. As a result, energy, commitment and achievement are all liberated.

Other than heroic journeys of private self-transformation, which while possible, are not a high probability for the majority of us, the major transformational tool we have is authentic communication, anchored in relationships that both nurture and constructively challenge us.

The Four Tests

So how can we improve relationships and thereby starve passion killers of their required oxygen? By this we mean rote, mechanical, artificial and often disingenuous interactions and suffocatingly superficial relationships. There are four tests of healthy, passion-fostering relationships, the type that enable practical innovation and exceptional results. Each test implies an accompanying strategy.

The first is, do we tell the truth early, openly and courageously? The key idea here is to learn to speak the truth in a way that builds other people, to speak the language of possibility as opposed to "you can't," to offer creative alternatives, and to enroll others as we suggest things.

So if Sally says: "John, your proposal makes no sense. Let me explain why." John is unlikely to be thrilled. In fact, he may prepare to fight for his idea.

But Sally can say with far more grace and yet with equal candor: "John, I'm worried that the proposal won't get us where you and I both want us to be. I may be misunderstanding you. May I share my concern? And then together we can find a way beyond that so that we can make this work."

People often speak of "brutal honesty." We do not see the necessity of the combination. Honesty is not brutal. It is the freedom to re-invent "what is" and to help each other really win.

The second test of robust relationships is do we consult early enough, when ideas are still in development, before there is excessive emotional attachment to them? Are these ideas frequently improved together, even transcended? In short, do good ideas routinely get better in our company, and is more energy spent on consultative co-creation rather than frenetic advocacy and after-the-fact critical cross-examination?

The key idea here is to realize that we will only frustrate ourselves by ramming ideas down people's throats. Moreover, the people who can activate our ideas can also shut them down, or seriously frustrate them. There are real benefits to making it a discipline to invite an early contribution from our colleagues, to get ideas from them sooner, to get challenges surfaced earlier, to get other people's perspectives and priorities factored in while we're still hatching our plans. There are two benefits:

1. We don't have to worry about being blindsided later on.
2. The idea is not just "my" initiative: it has joint ownership and collective responsibility.

Moreover, by also volunteering such assistance to others with their projects—not invasively but as supportively as possible— we take a stand for the establishing of this culture of being committed to each other's success. As the saying goes: "Bad teams work against each other; good teams work with each other; great teams work *for* each other."

It sounds glib perhaps, but it is profound and penetrating in action.

The third test of empowering relationships is to ask whether once our action is aligned, do we move fast from decision to action?

The real test of speed, as Carlos Ghosn of Nissan pointed out during his turnaround of that company, is not the speed of decision-making, but the *speed of action-taking* once a decision has been made.

The strategy above, or proactive consultation, will certainly help. But there is another aspect. Have we gotten to know each other? Do we know and trust each other? Can we ask each other for help? Do others ask us for help? Do we have a common purpose?

If our relationships are honest (see test one), then once a decision is truly taken, there should be few impediments to concerted action.

The key thought here is to invest time in building relationships (beyond even just consulting on issues), so as to both be appreciating and constructively challenging each other as a way of life. And then we will not only share our embryonic ideas early, but also our anxieties, or glimpsed obstacles, or perceived impediments to success. The strategy, if it can be called that, is to "talk" and thereby to truly *relate*. Rather than putting on appearances for each other, we are then emboldened to face what is before us. Rather than evading evidence of challenges and crises, our energies then shift to facing them and transforming them.

Meeting crises early, discerning a crisis well before it fully becomes one in fact, is both a hallmark of mental health overall as well as of leadership and team effectiveness.

The fourth and final test: are we more or less than the sum of our parts?

Powerful collaboration is highly challenging. There has to be an incentive to do the heavy lifting emotionally so to speak. There has to be a reward or promise large enough for us to take on our own demons and to grapple with listening deeply to each other with genuine curiosity rather than defensiveness.

So we need to commit to expansive goals derived from our vision and corporate purpose. But these goals need to have immediacy, vigor and incontestable attractiveness from a business standpoint. And these have to be goals that are ecumenical enough, far reaching enough, that they are impossible to achieve simply by aggregating the effort of individuals. They need the true multiplier effect to productivity, imagination and will that can only come from a real team.

These aims have to be larger than our addiction to our own comfort or even the siren song of our own vanity. We have to see a bigger "win" for ourselves, our team and our company from fulfilling such goals.

Here are three examples of such far reaching goals.

A client of ours is committed to "attracting higher end customers who become our evangelists." There is no way to tackle that seriously from a silo perspective.

Another said, "we will retain and attract and nurture the very best talent... we will become a talent magnet." Again, no department can achieve that. It requires the interplay of everybody.

A final example, "We will raise both profitability and customer satisfaction in these key segments." Note, this commitment extends beyond boundaries and demands the synergy of a team of talent. Such synergy is impossible without vibrant, honest relationships.

Let's Review

So, to remove passion killers, first we have to repair, restore and recreate our relationships. As they become authentic and vibrant, passion killers will wither.

Having (re)created healthy relationships, we then will face the truth, improve ideas together, act with alignment, and become more together than we are apart. If we do that, passion killers either won't form, or will be eliminated—fast!

All this sounds good. Still, we are left with a quandary. Even if we agree that the great restorative would be healthy, productive relationships, would not our global lack of success at effective communication give us some grounds for pessimism? In other words, why should we think our company, our teams, will experience a different outcome from all the other companies and countries that have failed?

The truth is that relationships are more likely to flourish if some key bedrock aptitudes are insisted upon from each team member and therefore become prevalent throughout the organization.

The reason that deep relationships are forged in intense external crisis (say survivors huddling together after an earthquake, or volunteers bringing aid to disaster victims) is that the extremity of the situation allows for virtually no other option than to move beyond agendas and come together.

More positively and more productively than in a situation of devastation, we need to create and usher in a positive crisis—a positive crisis that provokes us to re-invent our capabilities so that we can deliver our largest corporate aims and challenge our potentially stagnating status quo.

Grappling honestly with what this will require in terms of interaction and partnership, and seeking to bring this online into our shared everyday behavior will take us almost inevitably to our "last resort"—effective communication and authentic, creative relationships.

We will know we have made it when after some time our "last resort" far more frequently becomes our "first stop."

The next section of the book outlines the **passion liberators** that can make this so.

CHAPTER 4

PASSION LIBERATOR ONE:
"INTO ME SEE"

The first passion liberator is intimacy. Creating appropriate and enabling intimacy between team members and colleagues liberates passion, productive energy, creativity and more.

Just reading this may knock many for a loop. Intimacy? This conjures to mind for many personal romantic relations, not productive business collaborations.

However, that is because of how we've been conditioned to think here. Emotional intimacy between couples can indeed liberate and deepen physical intimacy between them. But emotional intimacy at work liberates and deepens understanding, synergy, effective interaction, purposeful debate and powerful connection.

In fact, leaders around the world know this. We are fans of Allan Leighton, the tough-spoken current chairman of the U.K.'s Royal Mail where he has turned around this once-ailing enterprise. Mr. Leighton's recent writings on leadership draw on not only his practical experience, but also that of business titans like Terry Leahy who runs the enormously successful Tesco's in the U.K., Sir Christopher Gent, chairman of GlaxoSmithKline, Brent Hoberman founder of lastminute.com, Perween Warsi (Britain's "curry queen") and even Rupert Murdoch.

Fascinatingly, high on all their lists of necessities for leadership success are people and teams. Fine. But consider what that really means. "People" become powerful when their talents combine *into* and *multiply through* teams. All these leaders speak of that. But what enables people to become teams? Certainly there are many skills and attributes. But underlying all of them, arguably, is knowing the mindset, heartset, values, beliefs, priorities, sensitivities, talents and even shortcomings of the people we are on a team *with*. It is hard to "team" with people we don't know. And it is hard to be passionate about working with people we neither understand nor care about.

So, intimacy, in the sense we are referring to here, may be rewritten as "into me see." It is that essential insight into each other that endows any aspirations of team community with legitimacy.

Intimacy tops the list of passion liberators and is arguably the ultimate bedrock of empowering relationships. Because if I create intimacy I have gained a deep and authentic insight into the needs, challenges and strengths of those I work with and am offering them a corresponding insight into myself.

The relevance, and indeed the vital importance of such knowledge and insight become readily apparent if we consider the symptoms that attend the absence of this kind of intimacy. We can catalogue them fairly readily: alienation, fakeness and unhealthy factionalism. Let's look at each in turn.

Alienation

Absent a sense of connection to others, which is what intimacy fosters, we feel apart, isolated, cut off from other people. We become emotionally at least more like the cubicle drones that Scott Adams so ironically takes aim at in *Dilbert*. Gallup, in their survey of high passion/high performance workplaces, identifies the presence of valued relationships at work as one of the most critical preconditions for excellence.

We can hardly imagine relationships at all, much less valued ones, when we are alienated and isolated, and emotionally remote from each other, rather than constructively intimate.

And to those who still say, "But why do I have to have more than professional relationships with my colleagues?" We would ask them to look more carefully at the embedded assumptions in the question. Why does "professional" have to mean emotionally detached? And do we really want to spend a large portion of our lives being indifferent to people we interact with, who influence the quality of our lives, and who we critically depend on for the quality of our results?

What becomes clear is not that there is much controversy. It is just that we are nervous about the energy and emotional lifting this might entail. We are right to be slightly daunted. But that is not an argument against the effort.

That is why we call it leadership.

Fakeness

When we aren't connected in any meaningful sense, when we do need to interact, which is very often in organizational settings, those interactions will be tarred by almost endemic fakeness. As we can't be authentically intimate, then we have to guard our appearances. And the appearances we will invariably project will either be those that are considered "attractive" by the corporate norms of that organization... or some societal median that we think will make us "acceptable."

Thus, for example, everyone may feign a certain superficial positivity, hustle and bustle with apparent productive purpose. They selectively listen enough to parrot appropriate inanities and overall either just take positions that protect our own agendas, or which reflect the way the proverbial wind is blowing. Real feelings, ideas, concerns, passions and commitments will be the casualties of the prolonged masquerade ball that corporate communication so sadly devolves into when this happens.

As we work with leading global clients, from sectors as diverse as banking, telecommunications, home and personal care, shipping and logistics, food, IT, hospitality and more, one of the most persistent passion killers they all mention is meetings. If you probe a bit deeper and ask what it is about meetings that distresses people so much, it's fascinating.

People mention that meetings take too long.

We ask why.

They reply because people get off agenda.

We again ask why. Do they lack the intelligence to pursue a focused agenda?

After some dithering, people will answer that intelligence isn't the issue. It's easier to speak about peripherals rather than tackle the real issues.

When we again ask why. After some reflection, people will say it's because people are worried about the *ramifications of honestly discussing what really needs to be discussed.*

So it then emerges the problem is not meetings. It is wasted communication. Wasted, why? Because everyone is putting on a front and evading the real issues. And the reason meetings are loathed and contribute to "burn out" is because the same issues come up over and over, albeit in different disguises. And they come up because they never get decisively discussed much less tackled.

Fakeness wastes untold time, money (both in terms of the real costs in getting people together and the opportunity cost in wasted energy and time), credibility, and opportunity.

Unhealthy Factionalism

A sense of belonging is a fundamental reality about human motivations. We see it from the formation of cliques when we are young; in our desire to identify with a particular religious group; in our sense of nationalism and patriotic identity; our keenness to be with fans who share our enthusiasm for a particular sports team or musical band; and in our need to belong to clubs and associations that give structure to our interactions. We are community critters. Without human contact, people psychologically shrivel.

That is why one of the worst punishments we can inflict is called "solitary confinement." It may secondarily be for the protection of others we may injure, but it is primarily a devastating shock and therefore deterrent for human beings. Corporate cultures that discourage intimacy and community create virtual cells of emotional solitary confinement.

The absence of intimate relationships in corporate life means that we tend to satisfy our sense of belonging not through engagement with others but rather through our membership in the most palpable corporate affiliation we have—our function, or department. We are hired by functions—marketing, finance, sales, HR, research and development (R&D), among others. Our career is fostered by functions, and so we tend to become advocates for and operational cronies of our functions rather than vital collaborators and co-creators across the entire value chain.

There are many ramifications. For one, it serves to splinter corporate visions that invariably have to cut across fiefdoms and silos if they are to have reality, much less vitality. Internal wars blaze out of control. The greatest cost in most organizations is the time and inefficiency of pass-offs between departments. Without trusting relationships and an understanding of the other people involved, all we can do is fight our own corner.

But there is more. Without thriving relationships we also have the potential factionalism between hierarchical levels, between regional and global teams, with suppliers and much more.

Given all this infighting, we will hardly put our creative energies where they belong: winning and growing in the marketplace through literally taking our customer's breath away.

It is no surprise that one of the planks that Jack Welch fought for so passionately at GE was "boundarylessness."

Fostering Real Intimacy

If instead of alienation we have real connection, if instead of fakeness we have courageous authenticity, and instead of unhealthy factionalism we have vibrant partnership and collaboration, passion will be released instead of being trapped.

Let us stop here to underscore the point. We are not speaking of intimacy in the sense of everyone adoring each other, or being best buddies, or planning family vacations together. We mean that people invest themselves in sharing something of who they are and learning about others in the belief that if they are to work together productively; they have to know who they are working *with*.

Intellectually it seems vividly self-evident. In practice, sharing something of ourselves requires emotional energy. Also, to extend ourselves beyond our own laziness and comfort zones is demanding. However, the need to do it is inescapable if we consider the alternatives. And the windfall it offers in terms of energy liberated for productive breakthroughs rather than trench warfare is more than worth the temporary discomfort.

Unless our paradigm of life and work is that people naturally want to confound each other and do a rotten job, there's no way around having a measure of intimacy in our interactions.

Most people probably *don't* get up each morning wondering, "How can I make life as wretched for my colleagues as possible and do as grotesque a job as I'm capable of."

The more likely paradigm is, "I'd like to help, but I don't want to look like a fool. I'd like to do good work, if I could figure out how to make an impact and be recognized."

We accept that this may not sound heroic, not the stuff of epic poems. But those comments mean people are willing to be engaged. If we can bolster our will, most of us would prefer to befriend and deliver rather than bedevil and dumbfound. Why? Because life is better, more interesting, more fun, more rewarding, more satisfying, more energizing, and more *passionate* when we make these choices.

There is another reason for building close connection and enabling authentic sharing between colleagues. There are times many of us aren't at our best. We are down, depressed, distracted, depleted. None of this is conducive to our best creativity or productivity. Being able to share this, even briefly, and receive an empathic hearing, lets us move on. Repressed, it weighs on us. Expressed, it can be liberating.

I was working recently with the regional chairman of one of the world's largest multinationals. This team had worked on fostering openness and caring relationships as well as a tough reality-facing execution edge. They felt the two had to be symbiotic if success were to be sustainable. Emotions are the fuel of our performance energy after all.

Jacques shared with his team a picture of his son, who had recently broken his arm playing soccer. Jacques said, "Well, my son was amused that I was going to show his picture to several hundred people." Jacques went on to say, "I miss him. But I was feeling a bit down to be away from him, as he broke his arm just hours before I had to come to the airport. But I am sharing this to make a point. One, I wanted to share something about me with you. What I care about and who I am. But also, just having shared this with you, makes me feel better. And I can now proceed." Indeed. Being able to share and move on is fundamental to being human but the job still gets done.

So how do we foster such intimacy?

Two of the reasons we don't often share intimate details is because 1) there are scant occasions for such revelations, and 2) someone has to go first. And if we take the initiative, and people are spooked, we'll become a pariah as people recoil and pull up their emotional drawbridges so to speak, embarrassing us in the process. Let's therefore suggest a way in which creating intimacy can be a true team effort.

A Simple Approach—Sharing Our Mask

Please note we say "simple" not "easy." That is an important distinction.

And while what follows is a focused process, we do believe that that being more open and honest, can happen at any time, in very natural interactions and conversations. However, sometimes we need an accelerator, or even a catalyst. If that is desired, this is a simple process you can launch at any time.

We suggest you start ideally with the senior-most leadership team in the company. If you are not able to do so, because you are a teamleader, business unit head or further down in the organizational hierarchy, begin with your own team, wherever you have the greatest potential for influence and impact.

Taking a discrete focused period, say an hour and a half for a team of 7–9 people, we recommend you conduct an exercise called "sharing our masks."

Though it sounds esoteric, it is astonishingly pragmatic.

A "mask" is simply an appearance. When people don't know us, our mask is simply how we appear to them. Some of the appearance may be deliberate. This happens for example, when as an emotional or psychological fortification, we project an image. Usually that is done so as not to reveal our areas of vulnerability.

So we act confident when truly we need encouragement; or we project an aura of independence when we are really seeking supportive relationships; or we exude certainty when we worry that others might perceive our doubts as chronic indecisiveness, and so on.

We put on masks when we fear that sharing our personal challenges isn't welcome, would repel others, or lead them to draw unfair conclusions about us, or use the information against us in some way. Like a masquerade party, we put on behavioral and emotional costumes and assume alter egos. This requires a lot of energy and imposes a lot of stress. Actors are often worn out after a few hours of being fully "in character." For such ongoing portrayals, alas, as our masks, the curtain rarely comes down.

It would be so much easier, less stressful and far more enjoyable to go through life without masks. But as we have seen, we adopt masks for a reason and it is very hard to get anyone to confess this. After all, the nature of the charade is that we are vehement in telling/showing/presenting to others that this *is* reality. Moreover, in time, we even begin to dupe ourselves at some level. Therefore, it is far easier to approach masks in another way.

The other aspect to masks is that we can locate them by exploring where we are most misunderstood. And this is a readily accessible way in.

If you ask your team members to remember that communication occurs at the end of the receiver (not the sender) and that the message sent frequently *doesn't* equal message received (the very definition of miscommunication), then we are likely wearing a mask where people regularly draw conclusions about us that aren't so.

To elaborate, while the truly confident are refreshing because they are so wonderfully congruent (what they seem to be and how they consistently behave are largely the same), those who assume "masks" of confidence tend to overcompensate and come across as arrogant. And while the genuinely distinctive seem wonderfully at peace with themselves, those with masks in this area seem militantly eccentric or sulkily isolated. Why? Because *the act of masking leads them to exaggerate the attributes of the very thing they are seeking to display.* Just as faux pearls have a gloss and a glitter that is more "obvious" than those of highly cultured pearls like Mikimoto and others, as we are "masking," we *overemphasize*.

So if we ask everyone to consider where people most frequently misunderstand them, where the points of friction in interactions most often occur (the places where they tend to rub others the wrong way), and where they feel they are least understood and appreciated, they often point to the masks they are assuming. That is precisely where the message being received is fundamentally different than the message we would like to send.

Recently in facilitating such an exercise we came across a leader who everyone thought to be chronically indecisive. They wanted him to take a stand faster. As he considered it, he felt quite misunderstood here. He thought he should consult and enroll. But as we explored this, we found he feared doing things without being certain he had covered all the bases. An past boss had unrelentingly raked him over the coals when he didn't triple-check every nuance of what he was presenting. As such he now wanted everything gone over with the proverbial fine-tooth comb and to be fully ratified by everyone.

Realizing that the real issue he had to face was taking a call when he had clarity on the key facts, the key risks and the key rewards, he was able to shift his work style, his consultation, and the depth and nature of facts he demanded, to facilitate this. His team also knew, by invitation, that they could now flag this to him, if they felt they were excessively investigating peripherals while vital time was being potentially lost. "Unmasked," he could help himself and invite meaningful support from others.

Such a sharing between team-members is surprisingly fertile. It is enhanced if the leader goes first and courageously sets a good example of relevant, not excessive, disclosure. This isn't an emotional strip show; it's removing unnecessary and stifling layers that are giving rise to unhelpful and often inaccurate perceptions in others.

When we've conducted this exercise, it is fascinating to find over and over how "safe" it is to speak about how we seemingly appear to others, and to have others weigh in either to corroborate or fine-tune. Many times someone will say, "You know I'm fundamentally shy." In surprise, a colleague will reply: "Amazing!

I would have said you were very confident, maybe at times even a little pushy." And the person sharing will usually realize what has happened and reply: "Yes, it seems that's my mask."

Or sometimes the mask is the same apparent behavior taken too far. Someone may say: "I'm yearning to contribute but I want to give others a chance to speak." And a team-member may reply: "I wish you would jump in more, though. You seem almost withdrawn as if you weren't really involved." And right away a rich and liberating conversation can potentially be underway.

Once masks (or distorted and/or exaggerated appearances) have been shared, it is helpful to have a team agree to review mutual progress on communicating with fewer such distortions and more from our authentic intent and selves—checking in, say, at monthly meetings as to how each person is progressing on the "process" of communication, not just its "content."

You set aside say 30 minutes, and have team members report on how they feel they are doing with their masks, and ask for inputs from their colleagues. And the team can also reflect if their dialogues are now clearer, bolder, more authentic, more graceful and more effective. If so, let's share in what ways—so that this can be built upon. If not, let's understand what blocking factors are still in place.

If then the senior leaders repeat this process with each of their own teams and a sharing of "misleading appearances" (the antithesis of intimacy) ripples through the organization, a marvelous lattice-work of relationship-cultivating conversations will take place.

Facing and Transcending Defensiveness

About three to four months later, another related process can be kicked off which further deepens mutual insight, trust and even communication leverage.

Each team member can be invited to share his or her "defensiveness profile." In other words, everyone is being asked to talk about the areas where they are most sensitive, or touchy, which feelings they are least comfortable with (for example being challenged, or doubted, or cross-examined, or ignored, or being second-guessed). The person is then invited to share where he thinks his reaction comes from.

Not always, but often, there are some seminal moments from a person's past that were painful enough to have these fortifications lock firmly in place. These may extend back to childhood, but may also come from the more recent past—an overbearing boss (as in the example above) or a team that came apart, or a highly stressful project.

Usually other team members when they hear these descriptions from someone will recognize them, having seen them in action. They will realize how they may have inadvertently triggered these defensive reactions in the other person, or at least had the opportunity to watch them "explode" (when defensiveness is expressed outwardly at others) or "implode" (when a person shuts down, or withdraws, or seems to be seething within).

However, once the reaction can be named and shared, it is no longer nearly as damaging. Once we have, in psychological terms, "disassociated" from it (i.e. are no longer personalizing the reaction), we can look at it as a phenomenon, not an intrinsic part of us. We can see that it is a learned reaction. We can unlearned this and learn new options.

Once the team members understand what triggers the defensiveness, they can be more alert and hopefully communicate with more finesse and acuity. And the person who has been defensive can also become aware of what it is that has triggered his/her negative feelings.

Let's take an example. If I dislike being criticized for anything, then I will seek out non-challenging and pliant relationships. And if underlying this hate of being criticized is a deep-seated inferiority complex that I am trying to violently stamp out rather than face, then I may become almost pathological when confronted.

If my outbursts when I am challenged are volcanic enough I may train people to go underground with their views of me. They will talk *about* me rather than *to* me. Moreover, people will then tend to withhold ideas, or concerns, or even offers of help, since they don't want to walk through my emotional land mines.

Hence my growth, my relationships, perhaps even my career progress, will be potentially stunted by my fear of facing critical emotions.

Clearly we are painting an extreme portrait, but only to make a point. And frankly the above isn't a caricature at all. Such instances abound in high performers who are driven to silence an inner critical voice, and therefore can't easily abide many external critical ones.

The only way out of defensiveness, paradoxically, is to actually *feel the feared emotion*. As we experience it more openly, it can't terrify us as much. As we face it, we only then can take the necessary steps to move beyond it.

Ideally to achieve this, we will choose to confront our fears in small, contained experiments, preferably in a relatively supportive environment. And hence we suggest team members come out of this exercise with a shared commitment. Namely, to support and encourage each other in facing rather than ducking the emotions they are currently responding defensively to.

Two members of a senior team at a pharmaceutical company in Cape Town made a commitment to actually reach out to each other, rather than be deterred by the wall of silence they tended to put up when they felt their conclusions were being doubted. They also agreed to seek each others ideas much earlier in the development process.

Again, knowing what triggered the silence, and knowing that isn't the response either leader was proud of, but rather was an unfortunate reflex, they could help each other past their respective barriers.

A team that supports its members past defensiveness is a team that can as a result have more bracing, gutsier, crucial conversations that can move the company's performance powerfully forward.

What this shows is that everything we have talked about in this chapter isn't a "soft" exercise. It's "hard" work intended to produce real results.

The alternative is far less appealing. We would be stuck tiptoeing and tap dancing around each other rather than facing what we need to.

As with the masks, once a senior team has embarked on this process, and actually *follows through* with updates, affirmations and feedback for each other at agreed regular intervals, these conversations can be cascaded, team by team, layer by layer, throughout the organization. Waves of positive interaction and genuine dialogue will shoot through the workplace.

Sustaining Intimacy

We've just discussed ideas for igniting more intimate exchanges. Sustaining intimacy is even more straightforward. A senior team of a global multinational market leader in personal and home care products observed to a Sensei facilitator: "It really was as simple, after we'd had those first sharings about our 'masks,' to stop by and knock on each other's door, have a cup of coffee and shoot the breeze, check out some ideas, find out what was going on, offer a hand, or else just even see how the kids were doing. From such exchanges, such informal dialogues, we got to know each other."

And it is much easier to be passionate about work, when we like, start to trust, and even look forward to interacting with those with whom we have to partner with to produce the results we are after.

Summing Up the First Passion Liberator

The first passion liberator is intimacy. In this context, that means "into me see," an invitation to be known and an eagerness to get to know our colleagues.

Then, at the risk of sounding like a trite song, I can be me, you can be you, and what we're working on is not mutual camouflage, but making our interface as productive and as results-delivering as possible.

An early book on the psychological concept known as transactional analysis was called *I'm Okay, You're Okay*. I worked for years with best-selling author M. Scott Peck (author of *The Road Less Traveled*). Dr. Peck once quipped that in his clinical experience as a psychotherapist, it might be more accurate to say: "I'm not Okay, and you're not Okay... but that's Okay!"

We are all a work in progress. We are not "okay" as in fully whole, fixed, complete, and utterly competent. We are growing. And that is indeed "okay" as long as we can share that and work on it *together*.

CHAPTER 5

PASSION LIBERATOR TWO: THE RIGHT BULL'S EYE

Having established intimacy, we can then focus on the right priorities, actions and deliverables that will make the organization successful. That assumes however, that we have a clear set of priorities, actions and deliverables. Hence the second passion liberator is knowing and sharing the right bull's eye.

This is rarer than we might imagine. Earlier we alluded to Gallup research that revealed that having valued relationships is a critical ingredient of high passion/high performance workplaces. That same research also showed that clarity on what we have to achieve, and having the wherewithal to deliver it (in terms of resources, skills, support, effective processes) is equally vital. Yet in our global experience, it is often woefully lacking.

At conferences, Omar often invites delegates to conduct the following experiment. Mentally draw up what you feel should be your team members' most critical priorities and goals, in terms of daily application and focus (not the printed captions that have been broadcast as "strategies"). In other words, what you would expect them to be spending the bulk of their energy, imagination and time on? Then, without warning or preparation, ask each member of the team what his/her biggest priorities are and what he/she is currently spending the bulk of his/her time on. The results will be at the very least revealing, very likely shocking.

Most corporate visions and strategies are either so vague, or stay up on the mountain top, with scant translation down into the valley of daily lives and efforts. And disconnected from the *raison d'être* (reason for being) of the business, work gets sapped of vitality and relevance and/of attendant passion.

The scripture reminds us, "Without vision a people perish." Why should that be so? Because a key fact about human beings is that every bit as much as we are community seeking, we are also meaning makers. We are driven to invest what we experience with some significance. When that is absent, we have the perfect conditions for an existential crisis. This is when we wonder whether what we are doing matters, and by extension, at least to some extent, whether we matter as well. Working through such a crisis can be a healthy transition during various life passages, but it is not an enviable state to prolong in productive people.

Our drive to look for meaning or to lament its absence comes from the fact that we are not only conscious, we are self-conscious. That is both our curse and our gift.

It is sometimes a curse because we often tend not to get on with things, paralyzed as we are by our fears and perceptions of how we will be perceived as we are doing them. We speculate, hyperventilate, worry, project anxieties, fantasize and self-aggrandize. This alternate mental and emotional reality often intrudes on the actual facts of our experience.

So we often encounter leaders who feel they lack "the right stuff" simply because they have a pronounced perfectionist streak. Perfectionism is very often fear in elaborate disguise. If I refuse to do something until I can do it perfectly, which is clearly impossible if we are stringent in defining "perfection," then I have an excuse for non-action. Or at the very least, I will wring each act for every ounce of certainty before embarking on it, even if much more would have been achieved and learned by diving in and then learning to ride the currents of our subsequent experience.

Working with one such young leader who we'll call Jacques, it was heart-rending because he was courageous, caring, connected well with people, had ample dedication and much more. But his self-consciousness of all his own perceived flaws and shortcomings was so acute, that he literally put himself on the rack for every imagined fault. His bosses thought highly of him and just wanted him to step forth into greater leadership. His fear was that he would be found out any day, for lacking the requisite leadership mettle. Few, if any facts, substantiated this concern. But his self-consciousness overrode the facts.

Three years later, this young leader learnt to "ride" that self-consciousness which he tamed and learned to harness like a wild horse. That inner voice is now an occasional spur, not a readout of where he is in his development journey. Part of what has made the difference is helping him locate and take a stand for a larger future. He has had a bull's eye worth growing for.

We should also mention in passing that the tendency of self-consciousness to overtake reality in a negative sense will be found as a prevalent recurring theme in biographies of many great yet personally flawed leaders from those painted by Shakespeare's immortal words to those like Napoleon who almost shaped an era.

Yet this self-consciousness is also potentially a great gift because we can more constructively apply the faculty of self-consciousness to consider the nature of what we are doing. Self-consciousness allows us to imagine more than what is. Applying it, we can convert fear into energy; failure into learning; and we can, at times, even use the suffering as an inducement to go on. We can do these things when we think there is a reason larger than our immediate pleasure or pain that justifies our self extension.

Winston Churchill tapped this capacity to galvanize his nation. As an Oxford don said to one of us: "For all of his prejudices, and excesses, for all his anachronisms, during that period when literally everything was at stake, he told us who we were...and we believed him. And that meant everything."

That larger reason by which leaders summon their own greatest energies as well as those of their team is almost always a vision of the future and some true purpose for our efforts. Passion naturally flows when these two dynamics are present.

Think of Lance Armstrong, battling testicular cancer but armed with an indomitable will, fortified by a purpose of competing in the *Tour de France* and a vision of winning it, he went on to compete and went on to win seven consecutive times after his rebound and recovery.

Think of Walt Disney with serial bankruptcies, nursing a dream and a vision of making people happy in a very distinctive way, on his way to creating Mickey Mouse and thereafter, an empire of sorts.

It can be Sony, battling the perception in the 1950s that "made in Japan" meant shoddy goods delivered late and stating the company's visionary purpose as: to make "made in Japan" synonymous with quality.

But one thing we learn very clearly by such examples is that vision by itself isn't enough. A vision to be the biggest and best may excite the owners and shareholders, but it will not necessarily enroll anyone else unless it taps the larger human need to be a part of something that has meaning. We seek significance for our sacrifices and commitment—that's one key source from where potential passion comes flooding forth.

However purpose by itself is insufficient. "We will alleviate suffering" is noble but without some visionary specificity it falls flat. It won't liberate passion because it is too generic, very much like "be all you can be." Yes, fine, but to what end? So we need both something to aim for (a future we want to make real), and a reason to care about making the shot (a purpose that makes manifesting it worthwhile).

A visionary purpose, the overarching bull's eye, doesn't even have to be stated necessarily. Let us explain why.

This is Not a Mission Statement

A visionary purpose is not the same as a vision or mission statement. It is a living commitment, reflected in all the priorities, metrics and rewards of a company.

Lou Gerstner in his historic turnaround of IBM pooh-poohed stating a vision for a long time. He "uncovered" one however in transforming IBM from a computer mainframe company to a customer-obsessed enterprise solutions company. Today, IBM is as much a consulting firm as anything else. It no longer manufactures computers.

Creating a new market and industry, being pioneers in a new value-space, is a powerful vision and can become an exciting purpose to commit to. It certainly did for IBM'ers around the world.

Jack Welch also didn't have a ready statement and felt that wordsmithing one was not his priority as he took over GE. However, two collaborative visions of a sort did emerge as his leadership philosophy was fleshed out. One was to become the most productive company in the world. And in terms of market capitalization and value, he and his team did, indeed, succeed.

Welch also wanted GE to become the best leadership factory around. And again he has succeeded. As of this writing, more CEOs of leading companies are alumni of GE than of the Harvard Business School.

For Microsoft the visionary purpose has changed over time. Initially it was to put a computer on every desktop. It moved on from that to: liberating humankind through software. This last description is probably laced with some marketing hype. "Unleashing imagination globally through software while being the primary provider" (reflecting the desire to dominate markets) is probably a truer expression of the company's vision and core purpose.

Again, it is the reality, not our utterances, that people pick up, act on, and become passionate about.

At the other extreme, one can read the rousing words of GM and the Ford Motor Company and compare those with the slipshod and dispiriting reality generated. Toyota's words are more restrained, but their leadership and team actions, processes, rewards and systems, exuberantly express their ethos of operational excellence and their drive to be the world's largest automaker—something they have recently achieved.

For our visionary purpose to have real vitality however, our story, our stand, the visionary future we are inventing have to come to matter to others as well. Starbucks has devoted itself to being the world's café, to creating refreshment and conversation hubs. Doubtless they also have targets, both in terms of expansion and profit, but their "story" has had to matter to the lives of both their customers and Starbucks colleagues within the organization before these other things could.

For Virgin and its iconic leader Richard Branson who took on British Airways in the highly regulated airline industry and Capitol Records in the music business, among just a few of his quixotic yet overall quite profitable adventures, it was a David and Goliath point of view that came to define the business. But his perspective has always been delivered with enough splash, cheekiness, insouciance and imagination to captivate audiences emotionally.

The key insight from all of this is straightforward: people need something to aim at, and it has to be something that either intrinsically matters to them, or which they would be proud to have made happen. Again, "we have to create a cause not just a business." And this passion is further stoked if our customers and consumers *want* the story to move forward, in fact want to participate in.

So this is the first aspect of this passion liberator: sculpt a visionary purpose and make sure the entire organization is focused and geared up for its fulfillment.

But this begs several key questions.

- Do I just pick one?
- Is a visionary purpose the result of strategic thinking or does our vision actually hatch our strategies?
- Where do we begin, and how do we locate a visionary purpose that is truly congruent with both who we are as an organization and what we can become?

Happily these three questions are almost always more troubling in the abstract than they are in reality. While it is true that some luminary founders of fabled companies will tell you, "I had a vision, we never really had a strategy," frankly they are almost always wrong about this, except in their perceptions.

What's often true is that they didn't have a strategic *plan*, and that is a very different thing. An extensive plan is NOT a strategy even though planning departments and corporate bureaucrats would like to think otherwise.

A vision worth its salt IS an expression of a strategic insight. As any management expert from Michael Porter to Kenichi Ohmae will remind us, the essence of strategy is how to gain competitive advantage. That means being crucially aware of how we will differentiate our offering in the mind and hearts of our customers. A differentiation that matters to the market and confers a competitive advantage is what we mean by being strategic.

Now out of all possible strategies and positioning choices how do people select the right one? By finding the place where our corporate passion, our greatest talents or competencies, and a deep enough profit pool, overlap. Sometimes we arrive at this through considered thought. Sometimes, we intuitively know. But even that intuition is grounded in the understanding of this intersection point: where corporate passion, potential profits and our company's core competencies come together.

Warren Buffet probably never said, "Okay I can produce toaster ovens or go into investing." Steve Jobs almost certainly never thought, "Become a lawyer, or create a new form of computer design that will rock the planet." These very different geniuses were led into certain fields by their passions, their talents, and their sense of how and where they could be successful.

Now it may be that Buffet would be almost invariably led into something akin to investing and Jobs into computers and design by their inner drives and would then create companies around these passions.

But how, within those universes, would they and their organizations stand out and distinguish themselves? Deciding *that* was their strategic choice. Buffet and his team developed a "point of view" about investing, investing for the long-term and not going for temporarily "hot" stocks or sectors. Jobs wanted to make computing user-friendly, and Apple moved from there into augmenting people's lives not just their lifestyles (iPods and iPhones). For Jobs and his team at Apple, that fits in with who they are; their take on life, and where they deeply felt Apple could excel.

Difference Between Strategic Vision and Plan

Visions come from strategic insights. Strategic insights emerge from the intersection of what we are excited by, can excel at, and where we can most profitably satisfy the current or emerging needs of a market or niche.

So as a leadership team, take the biggest thing you believe you can achieve. Next, decide how your achievement path will differ from others (your distinctive abilities, insights and point of view), and be clear how to measure success and assure that you're taking aim at a market that can provide the rewards you are after. If all those factors are present, you have a strategic vision (though not yet a plan).

Once you have this strategic vision you need to bring it to life for your larger team. Specifically you need to help them connect with it, add to it, refine it, personalize it. If you can link their success to its fulfillment then truly you have a corporate visionary purpose.

Taking it still further, make your customers care about it, and want to be affiliated with it, and almost want to "join" your brand rather than just "use" it, and you've got a cause that really liberates passion.

Sometimes though, breakthrough visionary purposes are so ahead of their time that they will only galvanize the market once they become actualized and are experienced. It would have been hard to get people excited about a 24-hour news channel before CNN and its subsequent imitators became a part of our lives. No one was palpitating for a Walkman or cheering Akio Morita and company at Sony from the rafters to make it so. These were demands that were created from a pool of needs glimpsed through a visionary and strategic set of insights.

If you are trying to create a product or service that a potential customer couldn't possibly imagine needing—a Walkman, an animated mouse, or an all news channel for example—then the level of internal intensity and excitement behind the dream has to be greater. It has to be the equivalent of a Manhattan Project or a Kennedy-esque "moon shot." For IBM, for example, after the life-or-death crisis was averted during Lou Gerstner's time, it was e-business (a program to integrate business at the strategic and operational levels through technology) that filled this gap and continued to produce impassioned dedication.

So, given all the above, do not spend the bulk of your time on the precise wording. The words will evolve and become clearer as you live the intent behind them. Working with a major financial services company, Sensei found them fretting over the precise paragraph indentation, the placement of semi-colons and the pros and cons of various locutions as they grappled with their vision statement.

The Sensei facilitator suggested: "Spend 90% of your energy on aligning people behind the ideas which seem very clear and reassuringly converged upon. 10% can still go into fussing over the semicolon if you like. But don't do what a lot of companies tragically do, which is to invert the percentages. People will still respond to visions they can't state, but which they know and feel in their pores. Equally, people will sneer at elegantly stated visions which they know make no difference to how you operate and who wins or loses within your company."

Well before it was stated as such, Fred Smith's team at FedEx knew that "absolutely, positively the next day" was their credo; their commitment, and something to which they had pledged their finances, their credibility and their business lives. Living it was the ultimate statement of this vision and purpose. Only because of that, now when we hear these words associated with FedEx, do they really mean something.

Once a visionary purpose liberates initial passion, what maintains the momentum? "Must-Win Battles."

Must-win battles are choices of the three to five most critical arenas where we must compete, come through, innovate, deliver and execute par excellence.

We like both the concept and the phrase because it underscores the fact that we must make trade-offs and choices. If strategy is how we win and how we differentiate, a strategic plan should be our highest priority bets on how we get there. By distilling key must-win battles, by making these important choices and then committing to them, we create this strategic path.

Here are the must-win battles of a client we supported to pick their biggest bets—those that furthered their vision, delivered the profit returns they were after, and most complemented their greatest strengths and competencies. They include:

1. Win in China. Understand its various regional markets and compete effectively based on those insights.
2. Launch the company's top brand in India. Get the adaptation to the local market right and communicate and connect to "own" the niche.
3. Gain 25% overall share in Europe by focusing on Eastern Europe.
4. Fill the leadership pipeline with top talent, but from a truly global mix.

This last (people always end up as the "last" item for some strange reason) wasn't just a filler by the way. They truly felt they would gain a tremendous passion liberation advantage throughout their global team, as well as reduce their costs on expatriate packages tremendously (about $20 million in annual savings), if the reliance on hiring and promoting executives from Europe was reduced.

This list of "top four" must-win battles was winnowed after substantial debate, consultation and challenge, from an initial list of 10. The other six dropped off for various reasons. Either because their impact on the global results wasn't large enough (that didn't mean they shouldn't be done, but they could be tackled through smaller more focused projects and initiatives), or else because they were too "technical" and belonged better as key performance indicators (KPIs) for functional leaders (for example close down excess plant capacity in Asia or gain X% cost saving by having global ad buys), or simply because they were an amalgam of several aspects of the same problem that then got sharpened into the key points above. Once the list of four was agreed to, everyone was invited to sign on and commit to making them happen. This cannot be "commanded." It has to be done through a process of communication, engagement and enrollment. Of course finally, it can't be left as optional. But if the visionary purpose and strategic rationale are compelling enough, it shouldn't need anything draconian to get people to sign on.

Things Change

Must-win battles are not goals that last forever. They are usually selected for a two- or three-year focus period. But during that 24- to 36-month window, we must stick to our must-win battles, unless there is a seismic shift in the world that changes the very basis for the selection.

On the other hand, the tactical steps we come up with, our "plan," have to be corrigible, responsive to change and continually emergent. In other words, we do things, we get feedback; we course-correct and recalibrate; we continue to measure ourselves against the most relevant metrics for each must-win battle and (very critically) against progress towards our visionary purpose.

So what are these "relevant metrics" and are they really that important? Let's take the second issue first and ask ourselves this. How passionate will we be if we can't see where our efforts are leading, or if it seems that our actions and those of our colleagues in other business units or functions are mutually nullifying? The answer is self-evident. We won't be very passionate at all.

Here's an example. A major Sensei client wanted to see how aligned business units were. Taking a leaf from an oft-quoted management demonstration, we asked the CEO to list the top strategic thrusts of the company. He did so. In a separate room, we asked business unit heads to list their four to five biggest initiatives and projects.

Bringing everyone and both sets of lists together, we asked the chief operating officer (COO) to use a color code—red for things that were off strategy; orange for those that were neutral; and green for those that directly advanced it. She did so. And then we looked at the result. Exactly like the experience we had read about, the chart of business unit activities was awash in yellow and red.

People started chuckling. Not in shock but in almost knowing amusement. This actually surprised no one!

And so the pantomime continues. What we just described—commonplace as it is—is a collective version of the Emperor's New Clothes. No one dares tell someone in power that anything is wrong—not even that he is naked.

Why does this happen? There are two possibilities. The organization's strategies are so generic or bland or outdated that business unit leaders with profit and loss (P&L) accountability make their own choices, sometimes with admirable enterprise and daring.

The other explanation is that the strategies are never converted into what we call "bold courageous steps"—audacious quick wins or inertia-overthrowing acts of initial daring that break ground in a must-win-battle. Another explanation is that strategies aren't monitored through a set of multi-faceted measures (whether they are the balanced scorecard quadrinity of financial results; process results, customer satisfaction results; and learning/personal growth results or some others), and that there are no consequences for being "on" strategy or "off" strategy. In other words, the strategy then has no "teeth."

The incident we just talked about was alas not an instance of crusading unit managers rescuing the company from its strategic sloth. What happened was more prosaic and more typical.

There was a disconnect between plans and actions—fostered (again) by lack of real communication, trust, empathy, intimacy or vibrant learning and accountability dialogues.

It has been said that we don't get what we expect but what we inspect. What gets paid attention to, what gets measured, tends to get done.

That is right. And in fact some rigor is particularly needed when it comes to establishing the right measures for the right bull's eye because of what can be described as "the activity trap."

Most people have a predilection to "charge" when presented with some task, attacking the problem at hand whether it is the right thing to do or not. As consultants, Sensei often uses experiential "games" to simulate real-world challenges and situations. Invariably when we ask someone to build something, or uncover a solution, or manage a process with multiple considerations, before we've even fully explained the parameters, if material for the task is laid out, people dive in and start. Far from "strategizing," what they are actually doing is "tasking."

Often they realize too late, and after they've squandered vital time and resources that they should have taken a few judicious moments to really understand what success would require (i.e. what the right bull's eye would be) before embarking on their attempt.

This is worth noting because in microcosm this is the essence of how we so often take good intentions and siphon off passion from each other by literally inventing a quagmire. From post-war planning in Iraq to gaining sponsorships for a major event a company is putting on, we've seen over and over and over again the unwillingness to consider downsides, to evaluate risks, to consider ways to maximize the return on investment (ROI). We have also seen the unwillingness to prioritize the key actions, measured by key deliverables and based on the most critical indices of success.

Accordingly, we've seen massive effort, massive cost, near exhaustion, anger at criticism, because so much has been lavished and sacrificed sometimes for scant gain. All we then have is whatever is the least worst of the remaining options. This is passion destroying and strategic suicide.

So decide how you would know you are delivering your visionary purpose or progressing towards it. Pick the most relevant metrics for success. And debate them thoroughly not only to make sure that they are relevant, but also to guarantee they make evident sense.

That last comment is not as strange as it sounds. For example, one of Sensei's key clients is a major home and personal care company. For years they pegged their progress based on market growth. As long as sales were increasing, they thought they were doing fine.

But it turned out that they were losing share against their competitors. It didn't matter if they were growing 20%, if the market was growing 35%, or their major competitors were growing at 30% or more. Relatively speaking, while growing, they were actually moving backward!

And pick more than financial indicators. This is the greatest wisdom of the Balanced Scorecard movement which pushes us to create a holistic set of measures that reflect different aspects of competitive health. Financial indicators are lag indicators; they tell you how you've done. You also need measurements that are "lead indicators" and can signpost how you are likely to do. These include benchmarked quality of key delivery processes, the innovation pipeline, customer engagement, customer satisfaction measures, team satisfaction and competency building measures and other future-creating indicators of this ilk.

Once you've got the visionary purpose and the must-win battles, with macro metrics for the first and more micro and iterative metrics for the latter, each quarter creates some "bold courageous steps" that would lead to impressive momentum towards the must-win-battles.

And then over-communicate all of these like mad. Link people's advancement, bonuses, rewards and approbation to the measures you've agreed to, and ensure they are known and acknowledged to be utterly relevant to the end in mind.

Measures can truly backfire otherwise. In one of Omar's consulting projects, he was coaching a senior marketer, helping the person to truly take deep personal pride in all he was accomplishing, in order to get him to reconsider quitting in a snit over being under-paid. This senior marketer was being paid substantially less than colleagues who shared his grade level despite having been promoted from a country marketing director role to a regional marketing role to eventually becoming a global brand director for this famous, global powerhouse. Why? Because the company policy was to base your pay on what you would have earned in your home market, adding in an additional amount as a cost-of-living differential where applicable.

The marketer had come from Malaysia and given the cost of living there, he was now being paid almost 50% less than a colleague from Sweden. This was particularly passion-deadening because this Swedish colleague was a middling performer by all objective measures, was not delivering nearly as well, but was paid significantly more.

Not surprisingly, the Malaysian personnel was incensed. He was one of the company's superstars. He had delivered 30% plus growth as country marketing director and had gained share against their toughest global competitors. He now had introduced an entirely new product launch that was going to redefine the company's profit position globally.

Despite that, being Malaysian, he couldn't be paid more than the fixed amount, given the way the system was set up.

It is easy to understand why he was livid. And it took the energized support of his boss to take on the HR system to get him paid fairly. It was energy and dedication that should have been saved for winning in the market, not winning over HR.

This is an example of where a metric utterly undermines the expressed values of the company. The company stressed it was a meritocracy, and yet one of its key members wasn't being treated that way. Our metrics have to jibe with our most critical objectives and also with the values we broadcast, otherwise everyone from the organization to the people who work there suffers.

3M is a company that understood this in an important way over many years. It required that a certain percentage of annual profits come from products innovated within the last five years. This measure underscored 3M's commitment to being the most innovative company in the world. BP has a formal process called "peer assist" where business units that are clustered together are measured by how the overall cluster performs and where best practice sharing is institutionalized and the most successful are accountable for supporting those struggling the most. This makes their expressed value of collaborating for creating value, real.

Change management thought leader John Kotter says: "The greatest challenge of leadership is to institutionalize leadership." Quite so. And what we measure and what we reward is a primary way to accomplish this.

As we've said, our metrics proclaim our values in the things we actually *value in action*. One of Sensei's major clients in the global logistics business had a devastating year post 9/11. They froze all pay raises and bonuses. Business units who had outperformed on all their targets, and had hit record growth numbers, were numbed and pained. They shared with us that they had challenged their leaders asking why when the company had three record years, was the upside also not shared with those being asked to make sacrifices. A condescending smile was all they received.

Ghastly lack of transparency and intimacy, and wholly inconsistent metrics being applied led employees to conclude that the "real" bull's eye shifts based on whatever suits corporate headquarters (HQ). When they come to believe that, how much passion are they likely to bring to work?

So what needs to be done?

Everyone needs to be clear on what the organization actually values. Everyone also needs to know that what is valued will be measured and rewarded. Once all that is consistent, we must focus everyone on bold courageous steps that are necessary to assure a successful future; mixing in some—not many— projects that may be necessitated by short-term needs. And always, always, always, celebrate all progress and reward those who deliver in line with the purpose and who exemplify the organization's values.

Once strategy is clear, values should relate directly to its fulfillment. These shouldn't be moral values per se, but values in action as we've implied above. In other words, habitual behaviors that contribute to the overall success of the organization.

We can state ethical norms like honesty and integrity readily enough. *But here we are talking about "behavioral differentiators" that will provide competitive advantage to our leaders.*

GE had a wonderfully simple set: energy (personal), energizing (effect on others), edge (ability to take tough calls) and execution (delivering consistently). Those who lived those values, and also delivered results, would as Jack Welch said, "be hugged in the heart and wallet."

At IBM, to create a set of values that would become annual commitments for every leader that could be measured and coached, Gerstner boiled it down to just three things:

Win. Focus on creating value "out there," maniacally serve the customer and remember the "enemy" is the competition not someone across the hall.

Execute. Speed and discipline, no more obsessive perfectionism, speed to action in effective ways.

Team. Acting as one IBM; plain and simple.

A leading communications company Sensei assisted expressed their values-in-action as follows:

- Fast, decisive action.
- Creatively challenging in a way that leads to innovation.
- Delivering in alignment with others.
- Utter dedication to customer success.

Clear values-in-action are fundamental in recruitment, performance reviews, identifying learning and growth opportunities and much more.

Why All This is Important

The takeaway message from this chapter is clear: Envision, prioritize, measure and track the right and most relevant things. Translate priorities into bold progressive steps that are visible and accountable, and ask for the behaviors that will over time build the leaders who can deliver your chosen vision.

How will you know you have succeeded in doing this? The test of a living visionary purpose, of having the right bull's eye, is five-fold.

1. Is the bull's eye clear and compelling to everyone?
2. Do people know how they can contribute to them?
3. Do they believe it can be done?
4. Do they believe their growth in the company will be based on delivering against these objectives?
5. Would they be proud to have been part of achieving it?

A "yes" to each of these are the five open sesames to passionate, engaged contribution pulsating and coursing throughout the company. Take full advantage of them.

CHAPTER 6

PASSION LIBERATOR THREE: RADICAL CONVERSATIONS

With a measure of intimacy in place, with exciting, transformational bull's eyes to take aim at, we now need to actually engage each other to make our corporate goals happen. We say "corporate goals" because that is largely what this book is about although all these tools can add untold value to our personal lives as well. Either way, engaging with others in such a way that we can truly deliver requires what we will call "radical conversations."

What are they and why are they required?

A "radical" conversation is one that goes to the root of one or more of our issues, opportunities, or challenges. We can say we are having such a conversation "radically" when we are fully present and committed to achieving at least three things: alignment, commitment, and ideally, a breakthrough.

Once the bull's eye is clear and the foundations of good relationships are actively being strengthened, then a company progresses based on the quality, audacity, depth, imagination, and the courage of its conversations.

We can testify from extensive global experience that if you take two competitors who both have strong strategies and talented people, those who have the better radical conversations habitually and consistently will win.

Let us illustrate this with an example. Sensei received a call from one of the world's premier food and beverage companies. The HR director was clearly flustered.

"We have strong strategies, but somehow, for some reason, we are not able to deliver on them. They're not happening."

We agreed to spend three days with the organization's senior leadership team. Surely if we put all our heads and hearts together we could diagnose the root cause of this inability to convert strategy into decisive action.

As Omar arrived for the morning of the session, he found that the company's HR team was in a tizzy and railing at one of the Sensei support facilitators.

"What's wrong?" Omar asked.

The HR director said in an exasperated tone: "Your team member says we have to randomly assign the nine leaders to sit in groups of three at round tables."

Perplexed, Omar inquired: "Yes, that's a set-up we often use. What's the problem?"

Turning almost beet red, the HR Director fumed: "The marketing director and sales director CANNOT sit at the same table. And I suspect you'll move people around so everyone interacts with everyone else. Well it can't happen with those two. *They hate each other!*"

Omar wasn't sure whether to laugh or cry on their behalf.

Just then their CEO walked in. Omar nabbed him straight away and brought him up to speed on this uproar. The CEO seemed sheepish.

Omar said: "You asked us to run a session to find out why your strategies weren't being activated. And you tell me out of a nine person leadership team, two of them hate each other to such a degree that they can't *sit* at the same table? And these just happen to be the marketing and sales directors respectively?" Omar let the incredulity in his voice be heard.

Here was a multi-billion dollar, global *Fortune* 60 company, immobilized because of a relationship meltdown between two key leaders resulting, of course, from the numerous *necessary conversations that weren't happening.* Not only were they not happening between these two, but as the Sensei team confirmed, because of the acrimony, they weren't happening between their team members either.

Omar let the CEO know that clearly the "mystery" had been solved—the company either managed enough maturity to at least share round-tables or else abort what would have been a foregone failure. He, the CEO put his foot down. People were apportioned to various tables and the session kicked off.

Happily at the end of day three, the atmosphere had improved significantly. During one of the final exercises, feedback was shared among members. The sales director looked for several minutes at the marketing director. He let out a deep breath and said: "You… are my challenge. We have to learn from each other." And for the first time this was said appreciatively rather than in an accusatory manner.

What had happened? In the course of three days, they had been challenged, inspired, catalyzed and taught how to share several, long overdue, radical conversations.

We've said earlier that virtually every corporate pathology can be traced to dysfunctional relationships. We can now be more specific about precisely how this happens.

Every corporate impasse is littered with the debris of radical conversations *we don't have or have only superficially.*

This can be demonstrated by reviewing some terrifying statistics about the level of employee disconnect, apathy and willingness to leave their current companies.

Based on a Harris Poll survey:

- One-third of employees say they are at a dead-end in their current jobs.
- 42% of employees say they are trying to deal with feelings of "burnout."
- Only 37% feel that top management displays integrity and moral values.
- Only 29% feel that senior leaders are committed to advancing the skills of employees.
- Fewer than 50% care what happens to the organization they work in.

Can it be that all these companies are knowingly inflicting such anguish and bitterness on the very people they have entrusted to deliver their business results? Or is it more likely that key leaders are promoting disengagement due to the relationships they haven't built and the necessary, transformational conversations they are not having?

How Not to Listen

One of Sensei's other main clients, a global giant in personal and home care products, like many leading corporations conducts annual employee surveys. These "voice of the people" surveys are meant to provide a necessary pulse on how robust, fair, and inspiring corporate culture and leadership are.

The results over the last few years have been devastatingly bad for this company. One of the key areas lambasted repeatedly is "quality of leadership." The senior leaders concluded that meant that everyone *else* needed leadership training! Certainly this couldn't be feedback about how *they* were taking decisions; the lack of merit-based rewards, the paucity of time spent coaching and developing; or the cumbersome reporting lines and bureaucracy they had inflicted on the organization as they centralized many functions and operations.

Moreover, the senior leaders again weren't a team. Their exchanges were politically charged and most were vying for the CEO's job. They behaved cannibalistically towards each others' efforts, undermining and second-guessing, and locking horns as a primary communication medium.

People always heard things like "Director X opposes Director Y's initiative," or "that will really embarrass Harris, but then Stephen is always out to get him…"

When these leadership courses that taught stock leadership skills were rolled out, people were incensed. These courses had nothing to do with the real issues and this was a blatant and deliberately obtuse misunderstanding of what the survey results were really about. A senior finance leader told Omar: "It's an insult to my intelligence." Indeed it was, though perhaps more of an insult to his assumed gullibility and/or naivety.

Such consistently depressing results should instead have provoked numerous radical conversations across the length and breadth of this global organization. Action directly linked to the feedback should have been taken: visibly, passionately, and emphatically.

And this company is about to receive even worse reviews in the coming year, at a time when they are no longer attracting top talent in many of their markets and where head hunters are awash with CVs from some of their most gifted performers.

Corporate value is literally being destroyed or chased away because of the conversations *not* taking place.

Is it always this depressingly bad? No! We know of numerous instances of exemplary leadership turnarounds, leveraged through the effective marshalling of radical conversations.

Bob's Story

Let's look at one. Bob was sent by his U.S. head-office to lead the Middle East region for his company—a leading conglomerate. It is a company fabled for innovation.

Bob's team was composed of an American, a Pakistani, two Lebanese, a Greek, a Saudi, a Singaporean, and a Brit. It was a true cultural hodgepodge. The prior management team had all come from the same cultural background and had hired and fired like a Mafia clan—divergence from established norms was punishable by excommunication.

Bob had never worked outside the U.S. so he seemed a strange choice. But that was the precise thinking behind senior management's decision to send him there. Knowing there was significant diversity in the senior team already, Bob was sent in to bring the values of his parent company to this region. They wanted him to "ride into Dodge" so to speak and clean up the place and return this region to profitability.

Bob did a lot right initially. But results were still slow to come in and he sensed a growing disconnect with his leadership team. So six months after his arrival, he asked Sensei to help him engage his senior leaders. The Sensei team conducted one-on-one interviews with each member of Bob's team. Many were seething at what they perceived to be his American cultural blinkers; his "good ole' boy" enthusiasm, and what they felt to be his interactive insensitivity.

The challenge for the Sensei team was to convey this input to Bob in a way that didn't shock him into either second-guessing everything he did, or retaliating by exacerbating what was irritating and alienating people.

What happened is a fascinating "demo" of how to prepare, stage, conduct, and follow through in conducting a radical conversation.

The first step is to state a provocative context, or opportunity or future state. Omar said to Bob: "Your enthusiasm is refreshing (it was), people are turned on by your can-do zeal (overall they were), and your passion for winning is a refreshing change after all the status quo politics of the past (this was more than true).

"We are all however sometimes unaware of our impact on others. Is it worth it to you to hang on to these strengths without offending, shutting down or intimidating some of your key colleagues?"

Powerful Conversations

Bob was intrigued. He said: "Of course it is. But I'm not knowingly doing any of those things. Are they saying I am?"

"You're producing some unanticipated impact," Omar answered. "My question is whether your aims here are worth shifting some behaviors and ways of interacting around for so that people aren't working so hard to deal with them?"

Note, there was no blame stated, only a read-out of impact.

Bob agreed—after all who wants to be working to produce results while inadvertently knocking people for a loop, forcing you to then work even harder for those same results?

Once a provocative or compelling context has been stated, that then becomes the reference point for all subsequent conversations. Whenever someone potentially gets emotional, or takes something personally, the original context is referred back to.

Therefore as explained, a radical conversation requires an agreed to canopy, one *worth* flexing for and taking the high road for.

So much of the art of such conversations is framing powerful questions or statements. When working with a global finance team, we asked them: "Why should you all not be outsourced to contain costs?" Initially taken aback, they responded: "We know the company deeply and care about its values; if you outsource you'll get technicians not co-strategists."

We asked them if their real value was in these things, how much of their time did they actually spend as co-strategists, team collaborators, and value ambassadors?

They went quiet. And then their leader said slowly, "Actually, not very much."

So they had said their reason for being an integral part of the company was the value-added contribution they made. But then they conceded they spent most of their time dealing with the technical aspects of their jobs, things that *could* be readily outsourced. As you might imagine, we were deep into a radical conversation.

This same team, having made substantial progress a few years later was ready for something more radical, more provocative, and more future-producing.

We asked them this time: "How can you as finance business partners help *lead* your company to profitable share growth (their most critical metric for the success of their business)?"

They had moved from why they should exist, to how they could take a leading role in helping to take their organization forward. A new radical conversation was underway—and with it, abundant new possibilities. While the story of this team is currently still being written, they are now actively consulted as true partners by their organizational business partners and they are starting to truly *invent value* in addition to protecting assets.

Once a powerful context has been stated, the next part of a radical conversation is to give the person, or people, a real stake in the success of whatever is being contemplated.

Omar said to Bob: "What you achieve has to last. If we can get this right; this balance between what you have to do and how to enroll a very diverse and currently uncertain collection of individuals so they can do it alongside you; then you'll not only turn around this business but also leave a meaningful legacy."

And as Omar and Bob talked about the importance of this, and how critical it would be to have everyone firing on all cylinders, facing and possibly shifting some behaviors or past established communication styles was no longer very daunting. Stating what is at stake, and making this personal, summons the maturity and wisdom necessary to embark on a radical conversation.

In the example of the marketing and sales directors, in that initially awkward three-day meeting, the senior team members affirmed their vision to be the world's best food and beverage company. They realized that all their hopes, their dreams, their commitments, the credibility of their company, and their careers were being held up by the almost childish peevishness of two or more of their top people.

Once the gravity of what they were facing was apparent, and faced with that as an inescapable alternative, few will want to vote for a future that continues to destroy their own dreams.

What Needs to be Done

With a powerful context expressed and the stakes highlighted, a few guidelines are necessary as the conversation is launched.

First, we need to create a frame that affirms that our credibility here is staked on finding a creative way forward—not a compromise, but a *fresh design*. This requires everyone contributing to commit to creating the new blueprint.

Too often in our education systems and upbringing we are told the test of intelligence is winning the debate and finding what's wrong in the other person's position. While egotistically gratifying, it reinforces the dead-end as nothing moves forward as a result. *Creativity is finding a way not confirming a barrier.* And therefore it is to creativity that we must appeal, along with courage and a commitment to reality, in radical conversations.

So Bob looked at his key team members with an eye to producing a breakthrough, one that required them to create a better way of working. Instead of having them adapting to Bob, they needed to find an interactive rhythm.

Bob had one-to-one debriefs with each member and played back not the specifics of what any one person had said (as we kept that confidential) but the overall pattern of recommendations he had received. He acknowledged and appreciated how the interpretation could have been created. He also asked the other person if they would be willing to listen to his perspective—not to evaluate it, or agree with it, but to understand where Bob was coming from. And then they built bridges forward by agreeing on how they would work together from this point on.

In a team session that followed, we also did this collectively. Bob shared the brief he had been given by HQ and what they as a team had to deliver and how they had to communicate confidence and resolve and the ability to execute, in order to regain trust from global bosses.

He made sure that the reality wasn't sugar coated. He explained his own drive for the turnaround emanating from a desire to see this region pave a future far richer than its troubled past.

He thanked them for letting him know how he was coming across. And together they decided to create a new way of working that, while on the one hand wasn't like the cliques of the past, but on the other didn't need the bombastic excess that didn't go down so well in the Middle East.

A radical conversation is not a surrendering of who you are. Rather it is *deciding who you are* and being willing to flex everything *but that*. So Bob retained his energy, his humor, his drive, his passion to win; even his gregarious effervescence. However he toned down the public ribbing he gave people (for a while anyway, until the whole place learned to lighten up a bit); he took people more into his confidence; he consulted and enrolled rather than just announcing and charging. And over time there developed a team of co-leaders standing right beside him in delivering growth.

When Bob left three years later, the troubled operation was posting double-digit growth and had become a benchmark in leadership development, customer service, and sales focus for the global organization.

As we mentioned in our discussion of HP and the World Café methodology, one conversation can produce a breakthrough, but it takes an ongoing relationship to sustain that breakthrough. Bob and his team continued to dialogue, to converse, to mutually challenge AND increasingly to mutually affirm. Relationships are built, one conversation at a time.

There are four psychological and emotional settings as we engage each other. The first two are destructive to radical conversations. The last two are wonderful fertilizers of them.

The first setting is denial. Out of fear of what we will have to share, face or expose, we deny there is an issue, or problem. Or if it cannot be denied, as in the case of the food and beverage company, we deny we have anything to do with it. The problem is solely caused by someone or something (market conditions for example) else.

The only way out of denial is to bombard ourselves and the person or team with data, feedback, impressions, results, impact from as wide a pool of stakeholders as possible. This jolts us out of the first rung of inertia and avoidance.

Practically speaking, if you are participating in a radical conversation, begin by sharing feedback you've collected about ways *you* may have been denying certain aspects of the issue. Ask the other person if he has any additional perceptions to share about you in this regard. Having already gathered some views, you are unlikely to be emotionally unnerved by what you hear. It is far more likely that it will be a reconfirmation.

And what follows from this naturally is that it is very likely that the person will then say, "Well I'm sure I deny various things too." Hopefully, if the feedback gathering has been agreed as a foundation-laying, you'll have some of that data. Or else you can say: "Would you mind if I share what I've observed about you?"

Having had an opportunity to give you input, it will be difficult for the person not to hear you out.

When you start speaking, do what Omar did with Bob: speak in terms of "opinion," "perception," and "impact" rather than making conclusive statements about the other person (such as "you **are** too pushy" or "you **can't** confront others").

The second setting is defensiveness. We tend to aggressively respond when we are accused of being culpable. We counter-attack.

While sharing similar attributes with denial, this is more militant, aggressive denial. It seeks to make engagement so uncomfortable that people may just withdraw, or go along, or skirt the person's sensitivities.

Team members and leaders have to expose defensiveness. The best way to do so is to share the impact of the behavior. You do this by saying something like: "John, you say you're not defensive. Here's what does happen though. You often drown out what the other person is saying with the volume of your voice rising as you do so. People pull back and draw the wrong conclusions about you."

And if John is smart enough to ask "which people?" it will take leadership forthrightness to say as gently but as clearly as possible, "Your team John, including me."

Here's another example of how to deal with the situation. Sue says: "It's not that I don't have initiative, you're micro-managing me and crowding me." She says this every time a senior colleague challenges her. Again, just speak to her in terms of impact, not intent.

"Sue, if you are confident that you are being micromanaged, then we should be able to talk about it without either of us getting upset. When you get upset, it creates the impression that you don't like being challenged. It's then hard to hear the real point you may be making."

Again, we will be better able to have this conversation if we have proactively elicited feedback about our own defensiveness and have invited our dialogue partner to also share their perceptions and views about us. You can then say: "Thank you. I can see why that must be difficult. It's been occasionally difficult at my end too. Could I share that with you?"

Again, done with respect and a commitment to the relationship, you are likely to be invited to proceed rather than to be shut down.

If we can move together beyond defensiveness, we can move to the next setting: curiosity. Curiosity is the beginning of openness, a first step to creativity; it is a willingness to re-invent the current status quo. As soon as we can shift the conversation to a future state we want to collectively bring into being (see the upcoming passion liberator for a full discussion of how to do this), the shift to curiosity is natural. We want to manifest this future and wonder how it might become possible.

We arrive at fresh design by focused, constructive, and purposeful wondering.

Then we use current obstacles as kindling for our imagination and innovation. The threat of being outsourced led the shared services division of a medical services company, to create new service partnerships with all their internal customers and to re-imagine the division as a "professional service firm" (kudos to Tom Peters for his wonderful insights on this) with just one client—the medical services company.

They decided to build a brand, fine-tune proprietary methodologies, develop intellectual capital, commit to the success of their (internal) customers to deeply understand their problems, and to innovate new processes and solutions to respond to them. And very critically, they developed the emotional skills to empathize and become truly trusted advisors rather than mere expertise-specialists.

Their internal appeal skyrocketed and the economics of outsourcing couldn't compete with the remarkable value being experienced by the business units they were supporting.

As a radical conversation shifts from curiosity to fresh design, one way to keep the powerful momentum going is to volunteer personal accountability for the changes being discussed. Agree how these positive changes can be tracked and commit to finding out how you are doing. And then invite the other person to also accept accountability and gain an agreement whereby you can also let them know how they are doing.

Once a month catch up with each other, or whenever a critical "moment of truth" occurs, and ask "How did I do? What further suggestions do you have?" A great radical conversation leads to the parties becoming each other's coaches in the area being discussed.

Track the commitments zealously and ensure ongoing dialogues and check-ins are planned. Again these should be undertaken with *curiosity*. "How am I doing?" should be a statement of real curiosity because you are asking how you are coming across to another. Then the movement to still better design and action happens quite readily.

During radical conversations, one warning looms. While it is important not to try and finesse what you are saying too much, we do need to make statements that potentially invent a larger future and which open up possibility. The next passion liberators are about precisely that.

Applying This Passion Liberator

Make a list of two to three impasses at work or even at home. Lurking behind each of these is a radical conversation that you need to have. Pick the top two to three such conversations that would be most impactful and transformational. These will be usually those that if successful would make a major impact to one or more of the critical success factors of the business. Sometimes the impact would be direct, as when a particular problem like time to market is tackled and improved upon. Sometimes the value received will be indirect, say when two critical relationships—like the sales and marketing directors of that food company—are then able to put their energies and agendas together not just once, but in a multitude of ways each day.

Having identified the conversations, ask yourself who you can consult, what preliminary dialogues you need to have, to prepare the ground for this radical conversation.

If you are estranged from the other person, get a boss or trusted colleague involved. Or simply make that person an offer, stated in terms of outcomes he/she is dedicated to. Present yourself as a passionate ally if you two can co-create a better way forward. Very few will refuse such an invitation. And if the invitation is refused, then indeed you must get help. You can't be on a team with someone who refuses to communicate with you.

Then act on these guidelines: create a provocative and yet liberating context, specify the stakes, ask for input about how you are coming across (stay "curious" rather than defensive, ask questions so you can understand their perception even if you don't agree with it). Also share the impact your team mates have on you; wonder together at new options and possibilities; brainstorm new paradigms and designs and behaviors; volunteer accountability and ask for some in return. Always agree how mutual improvement will be tracked. Catch the other person doing it better, not just "right" (progress is what we have to enthusiastically endorse), and with genuine curiosity let each other share at regular intervals how well we're making it happen.

Passion is liberated by such conversations because they take us past the recurring problems that have continued to stymie us. They also open up new pathways to re-invent previously ossified relationships. And they help us translate what has been holding us back into a larger, more compelling future, with shared accountability.

What we must learn next is how to ensure that these conversations, and we along with them, can create the future rather than just berating the past or bemoaning the present. We turn to that now.

CHAPTER 7

PASSION LIBERATOR FOUR:
PROTECTING POSSIBILITY

Radical conversations require that we stay curious as we move towards fresh design. We need to face reality, but we need to do so in a way that protects possibility; that keeps the opportunity for a larger and more exciting future in view. Keeping possibility alive, as we interrogate and embrace our challenges and opportunities respectively, is the next passion liberator.

But as implied above, the first step of protecting possibility is for us to make peace with reality. It doesn't have to be a permanent peace—but a *détente* that allows us to creatively find paths forward.

How you do that is fairly simple. We face "what is" squarely. We meet head on *our feelings about this reality*. If we deny those feelings, we stifle the very potential passion that can fuel us forward.

Let's use the parenting example again to show how this plays out in practice. A father has heard his 17 year-old daughter asking questions that raises his concerns about whether she is sexually active.

The "official line" the parent will adopt is to say his primary concern is to ensure his child is educated about consequences, is making conscious choices, and practicing safe sex. However, in truth, this parent's emotions about his daughter's sexuality are far more complex, as are those of most parents. The father's emotions combine sadness, worry, vestigial prudishness, moral twinges and a desire to make sure she isn't hurt.

If the father denies all these complex currents, he will talk to the daughter on the surface: solely about "safety" and "responsibility."

She will wonder why if that's all he is taking about; why her dad is being so overbearing, so domineering, and so volcanic. The result will be *incongruence*—a mismatch between what he is saying and the degree of evident turmoil and agitation within him.

As the parent denies there is anything more, and the daughter palpably feels there definitely is, she is unlikely to feel welcomed to share the full range of her own feelings, desires or experiences. Rather than mutual engagement, rather than a relationship-fostering, passionate conversation, they will speak *at* each other rather than *to* each other. In time, they may cease to speak at all on such matters.

The Power of Shared Emotions

We cannot speak usefully when we stifle our emotions. So often when it is something controversial or even outright contentious, what is really creating the controversy or the contention are the underlying emotions. When those can't be directly taken on, the conversation—as we've suggested before—becomes trivial if not farcical. However, we invite a reciprocal sharing from others when we *can* confess our emotions without trying to make them sound virtuous or inevitable but with a degree of humility and openness.

In company settings, we see this all the time. A direct report chafes at the "overbearing" management style (in his perception) of his boss. In truth, his own feelings may be a desire to show how good he is; an anger perhaps at dominant father figures; and a partial insecurity about his own ability as a leader. If he were open to all his feelings the two could have a fruitful conversation about how he needs to be coached, communicated with, and constructively held accountable by his boss without feeling micro-managed.

By denying these feelings and claiming it is all about the content of his "role" as a brand vice president and his boss' "role" as a regional vice president, nothing can move forward. We are not suggesting this brand VP say to his boss: "Well, I have issues with father figures and am insecure about myself as a leader, and that is what is causing the conflict here."

In a wonderful world, that could happen without anyone feeling his standing has been compromised. But we don't live in a world where that is likely to happen any time soon.

In the real world, the communication would probably sound much more like: "I often find I'm uncomfortable when someone oversees what I do as consistently as you do. I'm trying to find my way as a leader, to find my own leadership style, and it's hard to do in your shadow. Can we discuss how I can get your guidance, and you can have the oversight you need, without this happening?"

Notice this is the language of curiosity, of wonder, of open questions that can creatively lead to designing a new pattern of interaction. But it comes from being aware of all our feelings as we take on reality.

This requirement of being present to all of our feelings about the way things are is far from easy. In fact, to fully engage in this practice, we have to go further. We not only have to be present to all our feelings, *but we must do so without resistance*, without throwing a tantrum that the reality exists. It may not be the most pleasant reality, but being infuriated by its existence means precious energy is being siphoned off in pointless anger and stress. After all, all we really can ever transform is the reality in front of us.

If we "resist" our feelings, we miss the opportunity of exploring both their full, enabling power as well as their ability to fertilize our imagination and creativity.

Embracing Challenges

So the aim is "presence without resistance." This is the pathway to innovation and creativity. Otherwise our creativity and our emotional energy go into self-deception and suppression. The capacity to be present to everything that is happening without fighting the fact (if it is already in existence), liberates possibility. The struggle shifts from coming to terms with what has already happened, to reinventing the landscape of both reality and potentiality.

Here is an example. As a skier, we've experienced what happens when we tense up and try to "pull back" when encountering icy patches. Down we go! We destabilize ourselves, throw off our form, and ignore the ice as a conduit of our forward motion. When we relax into those patches and let them carry us forward, we frequently find ourselves moving quite elegantly through them. A fellow skier once commented: "Mistakes are like ice, we have to let them take us forward."

Once we include mistakes in our definition of performance, we can admit them faster. That makes it easier not to perpetuate them, and it allows us to "stumble forward," if stumble temporarily we must.

It sounds simple. So, why do we find it so difficult to do? Our resistance comes at least partially from our lust for acting as if we "have it all together." We become addicted to the *appearance* of competence rather than being willing to work to earn that competence. We then forget the uphill glory that attends all types of genuine leadership growth.

Benjamin Zander, the conductor of the Boston Philharmonic, and an enthusiast par excellence, tells the tale of the great composer Igor Stravinsky who once turned down a bassoon player who was "too good" at rendering the opening to Stravinsky's *Rites of Spring*. As Zander explains, that music is seeking to convey the "first crack" in the icy grip of the Russian winter; it is meant to be almost heart-stopping, a perilous moment of excitement.

"This player," Zander says, "while technically perfect, couldn't convey that exquisite yet aching moment."

He tells another related story to elucidate this point. When hearing of a difficult moment in the violin concerto, Stravinsky said: "I don't want the sound of someone playing this passage, I want the sound of someone *trying* [emphasis added] to play it!"

Leadership is like that. Leadership is frequently the "sound" and "sight" and "feeling" of someone *trying* to play it—seeking to live it, yearning to fulfill his/her potential for contribution. To have any chance to do so, we have to face what happens as we try, without resistance. Only then do we shift from being in a defensive position of trying to avoid mistakes into the curiosity stage—one of learning and genuine growth.

Another complication is that often we forget that we treat our "assumptions," our "projections," and our "conclusions" as reality. By doing so, we ignore the multi-faceted tapestry that reality so often is.

A persistent rain we face on a trip can sour our journey while being a god-send for the local crops. A forest fire may injure an ecosystem, only to later allow it to renew itself with vigor. A tempestuous argument with a spouse can create "space" for fresh feelings that can both excite and empower their relationship. A flight delay can have us late for a meeting, while allowing us to find and spend time with a book that sparks a breakthrough for us and our team. It would be wise therefore, to avoid investing our rush to judgment with too much credence.

An old story makes the point. A student goes to his Rabbi. The Rabbi instructs him: "When you get good news, thank God; when you get bad news, thank God". The student thanks the Rabbi. But then mulling over the instruction, he asks how he is to separate out "good" news from "bad" news. Smiling with delight, the Rabbi says: "You are wise my son. So, just to be safe, always thank the Lord."

We can state this in slightly less exalted language for today's leader: Look at everything with the eyes of possibility, grateful for the opportunity, and hopefully the capacity to do something with it. But get to that moment FAST.

And as you get to that moment, understand that how you see the world will color everything else. The following, possibly apocryphal, tale illustrates this.

As people approached Athens they would often seek out the famous sage, Socrates.

As the tale goes, a family approached Socrates saying they were thinking of moving to Athens and wanted to know if people there were good natured and friendly, welcoming and neighborly.

Socrates asked how the people were where they came from. They replied that people where they came from were negative, obnoxious, and quite horrible in fact.

"Don't move to Athens then," said Socrates, "people here are just like that."

Some time later another family happens by and asked Socrates the same question. He in turn asked them also how the people were where they came from. This family replied that where they came from the people were friendly and kind and caring. "Move to Athens then," said Socrates, "for people here are just like that."

The point is that in many ways we don't see the world as it is, but as we are.

Some years ago Omar was coaching a leader who was becoming exasperated by a young manager he had hired. The executive complained that this younger manager had built a "wall" around himself.

Omar wanted to see this first hand, so he and the senior executive walked down to the young manager's office where the senior executive repeated his comments—this time in front of his charge.

The young manager said nothing, seeming somewhat overwhelmed by the forcefulness of his boss.

"See?" the senior leader said, and he continued to deliver a variation of his rant about how non-responsive the young man was. Ironically, the more the senior manager interpreted the younger man's reticence as "wall building" the more, in his mounting frustration, he acted in ways that constructed the wall!

Face to Face with Reality

Facing reality means distinguishing between "what is" and our own conclusions, beliefs, and assumptions. This senior manager had characterized his young team member's silence or diffidence as him having "constructed a wall." You can almost sense the wall being erected in the passage above! As the young man didn't respond, the "wall" was confirmed in the senior manager's mind.

The young manager's reality may have been that his boss was an overbearing, impossibly demanding taskmaster. The more the leader ranted the more true this became in the younger manager's perception, and so the less incentive he had to express himself or to be more out-going.

Imagine if the senior manager had decided to dismantle the wall in his perception, and had simply noted what is. He could have said to himself: "A young leader I believed in is being silent and I'm frustrated that he won't communicate with me."

And also imagine if the young manager had thought candidly and non-judgmentally about the situation. He might say: "My boss wants to communicate, I'm not sure I know what to say, or how to say it, but I can see he wants more from me than I'm giving."

Imagine the richness of a conversation that could flow if it began with a real sharing of "what is" for each of them, the emotional realities above. We can almost sense the importance of the bridges that could be built if these inner feelings were shared and received with respect, curiosity, and real interest.

When we treat our own manufactured abstractions as the primary reality, we are kept from seeing the very things we need to see in order to achieve what we really want. This is true both in terms of business results as well as team evolution, and of course the interplay between them.

The even greater leadership danger is that as we keep reconfirming our own conclusions about "the problem," we then tend to pick those perceptions that conform to our prejudices. The mind is like a heat-seeking missile, the more we look at the world with this bias, the more "evidence" we will locate for our perception of choice. This is also why we notice a flood of Honda Civics on the highway soon after we buy ours, or a bumper crop of young infants the week after we've wheeled our own out of the hospital. As we can see, "seek and ye shall find" is as perceptual a truth as it is purported to be a spiritual one.

If we fall into this trap of, in essence, seeing what we hope to see, we run the risk of either creating strategies that don't address what is really needed, or else we begin to emotionally confirm a conclusion that the problem is insoluble. This is why rigorous, initially dispassionate analysis is *so* important. But, again, we are talking about dispassionate analysis coupled with *curiosity*, not denial or even defensiveness.

Moreover, as the evidence starts to come in and the tumblers of our mind begin to turn, we need to change the frame from "all or nothing" and begin to rejoice in even small wins that create momentum and provide evidence that increasingly affirms faith, possibility, and fresh design.

So as an example, you can join the crowd bemoaning the inevitable decline of audiences for serious theatre, or you can celebrate the sold-out performances of Bertolt Brecht's *Life of Galileo* at the National Theater in London and of Tom Stoppard's *Rock and Roll* (an exquisite romp of ideas and cultures that was a huge hit in London before heading off to Broadway). You and your pro-theater cohorts could park yourselves at the exit of these shows, thank people for coming, and hand out flyers alerting them to an upcoming performance of another worthy show. While you're at it, you and your colleagues could even give them a "special rate" if they bring their friends along.

If demoralized by what you perceive as the decline in classical music interest, you could join the throng of thousands that converge upon Mozart's lovingly preserved baroque home town of Salzburg, and then re-enter the world fully revitalized by the alternate reality of classical music interest that this most prestigious of European musical festivals conveys. And then create a club of friends who rejoice in life and friendship while attending symphonies.

The "slow food" movement started as a passion for freshness and real conversation among a small collection of committed connoisseurs. It has now become a global phenomenon.

We take a stand, we make a first step. We are open to all that happens; we accept and share our feelings; and we continue to be a prism through which possibility can shine.

So, once we accept reality and our feelings, we then empower ourselves to *create* fresh milestones that take us towards an enhanced, enriched, and more spiriting reality. All real leaders work with their teams in this way: as constructive co-conspirators to create possibility-rich frameworks.

Martin Luther King intoned: "I have a dream!" When we don't face and interrogate reality, we corrupt this to "I have a pipedream... a wishful fantasy at best." On the other hand, when we don't accept our responsibility for co-creating what *can be* through engaging our own and other's perceptions and feelings and frameworks, we mutate this into "I have a nightmare."

It's our paintbrushes and canvas though. We decide whether we face and then influence reality constructively or not.

Making This Real

A powerful tool that organizations can use to fertilize and facilitate this is called "the possibility focus." It builds on a tool for personal development called the "positive focus" by entrepreneurial coach Dan Sullivan.

The best way to understand this tool is through its most natural application which is in all kinds of meetings. Begin each meeting with a review of what has gone right since you last met.

Too often all we focus on is what has failed, or what the problem is. Reviewing what we've accomplished protects confidence, energy, imagination, possibility.

Then ask *why* it went right. We often say we must learn from our failures. And indeed we must. But we also must learn from our successes as well. Why did we do well here? How can we further leverage this?

And then ask "who should we thank?" If they are in the meeting, we have a chance to recognize and acknowledge that person, or people, in real time. If they are not present, the team can consider how to let them know their contribution was deeply appreciated. The "thanks" needn't be monetary or even time-consuming. But it should be personal, authentic, and heart-felt, never just ceremonial. Invest the appreciation with the emotion it deserves.

The second part of the possibility focus, once we've affirmed our progress and have celebrated contributions, is to then look squarely at what *hasn't* gone well and what we need to improve. But we need to do this in a future-focused way that protects possibility. So rather than looking backward excessively, once we've stated the deficit, we need to convert it into a future-focused commitment with energy going into making this future real.

So, let's say, during the meeting someone notes that sales in our top brand slumped by 15% in the last quarter. Obviously, we need to spend some time understanding why and getting to the root cause. But the moment there is clarity and we've made sure we've fully explored and understood the various drivers that produced this, we then need to restate a new goal. "Okay so in the next 30 days our commitment is to improve our sales results to return to plan. Let's discuss how we're going to do this and what it will take from everyone. Can we do better? Is that bold enough? Where can we create some windfalls for ourselves given what we've learned?"

However the conversation evolves, and whether that meeting is the right forum or otherwise, all attention, all energy, all focus, has to go towards endowing the future with the alternate, possibility-rich reality we are articulating and asking everyone to sign on to make it happen.

Please note, the possibility focus as a discipline for meetings will only work if engaged in consistently. And both of these aspects—the appreciation and the collective self-challenge—require energy and application. If done formulaically or in a pro forma way, they will deaden passion and possibility rather than liberating them.

One of Sensei's clients based in Asia put the possibility focus to the test. As a plant manager in Indonesia (he was himself Sri Lankan, welcome to the flattening world), when he encountered some initial resistance from his team towards this approach, he told them: "You can waste energy resisting this, or you can put energy into making this valuable. But we're going to do this regardless."

Within a few weeks, as energy surged as a result of following the "possibility focus" approach, problems got tackled far more proactively. It became a challenge to earn an "accolade" or to ensure a potential problem either didn't occur or a current one didn't worsen. Rather than hiding issues, they were broadcast, ventilated, debated, discussed, and dealt with. Rather than becoming defensive, given a good blend of affirmation and challenge, people rallied to the dialogue. In fact, the plant manager, Dinesh, started to have his next level leaders lead the weekly possibility focus meetings. They in turn cascaded it to their teams.

Three years later, Omar met Dinesh in Singapore. He took Omar aside and said: "That exercise, the possibility focus, is fantastic. I wanted you to hear this from me. It's been two years since I left Indonesia. The guys still continue with it. In fact, the team has taught two sets of plant managers after me the way to do it. And these new plant managers seeing their enthusiasm, and the results, didn't mess with it, they keep using it. That plant continues to be one of our model facilities, in terms of productivity, quality and safety!"

The message here is clear. Use the possibility focus with anybody with whom you have a recurring interaction. Begin by recognizing and affirming the progress made, understanding what has led to it, and thanking and appreciating those who have helped.

With that as your base, and always using a future focus, speak the language of collaboration and mutual accountability (as we learned in the section on radical conversations), and invite fresh commitment for delivering even stronger results together in the future.

Leaders who want to liberate passion have to ensure that possibility-furthering conversations are taking place each day. They have to ask people periodically, "So, what are you working on?" And then listen first to ensure that what they reply reflects the right bull's eye (passion liberator two); and that they are stating their efforts in terms of future-focused possibility-rich achievements rather than in backward-looking "recovery" or "maintenance."

Below are some examples of possibility-rich approaches:

- "We are trying to stop errors in processing" is far less possibility advancing than a comment such as "we are ensuring our processing accuracy returns to 95% or higher in the next two weeks."

- "We are trying to reduce our overdue receivables" isn't as invigorating as saying "we are aiming for improving our cash flow by ensuring we have no receivables over 60 days by the end of the quarter."

- A comment such as "we are ensuring top people *want* to stay with our company in overwhelming numbers" will ignite more creative imagination than "our goal is to reduce turnover."

This isn't just semantics. It's a matter of taking a stand for the future in a way that is powerful enough, expansive enough, that we, and the people who work with us, will be inspired to reinvent our current reality, and if necessary our own behaviors, attitudes, aptitudes, and actions.

To illustrate this, think about this. The great corporate leaders we all have read about have one thing in common with visionaries such as Albert Schweitzer, Nelson Mandela, and others.

Both great leaders and great visionaries *have the ability to be present to the way things are both in times of beauty and joy, and also during periods of challenge and frustration*. Both understand that we have to face, embrace, and then transcend what we experience and find ourselves facing.

In other words, to be alchemists, we may have to be chemists first.

Such leaders and such visionaries can look at the full range of both our challenges and our potentials, and never position themselves in any way that presents a barrier to creativity or to hope. That is what reframing our challenges into possibility creation is all about.

Mother Teresa was once asked how she could continue to generate her passionate devotion in the face of such seeming overwhelming futility. She answered simply: "God did not ask me to be successful, He asked me to serve." In other words, her report card grade was based on the people she helped, not how many were still suffering. Once again the focus is on progress, not perfection.

Nelson Mandela did not stagnate during the many years of his captivity. He taught philosophy to inmates and even guards while there! The jail came to be euphemistically known as "Mandela University." So great was the influence he exerted through the force of his ideas and example, that when it came time to dismantle apartheid, the government of the day knew it couldn't proceed without negotiating with a jailed prisoner who would subsequently win the world's admiration as President Nelson Mandela.

These are extraordinary examples, and most of us need not consider if we have the capacity for such exceptional forbearance, grace, or character. However, we can become "possibility superstars" and galvanize our own efforts as we interact with our teams, our customers, and our marketplace.

Using This Passion Liberator

When we keep carping on what "should be" instead of seeking to transform "what is," we show a true failure of courage. We also cannot be truly creative because we won't immerse ourselves deeply enough to truly discern what ingredients we really have, or what they might help us fashion anew.

Leadership is about transformation. But we cannot transform what we don't accept or face. When we decide to utilize this passion liberator by using approaches like the possibility focus, not only can we transform the situation, we can also transform ourselves.

So the first step is to ensure the possibility focus becomes a consistent discipline at everything from board meetings to review meetings with project teams and everywhere else throughout the organization. Virtually all conversations should have two elements: an appreciative and encouraging element as well as a challenging and constructively stimulating future-creating one.

Let's make sure all our performance reviews, our coaching, our mentorship, our team engagement express both of these symbiotic priorities.

This passion liberator teaches us that when we not only "accept" but even imaginatively come to appreciate "what is," then what "can be" shimmers all around us.

It is a precondition to creating the future we want.

CHAPTER 8

PASSION LIBERATOR FIVE: PROVOKING THE FUTURE

Armed with possibility, we are ready to take the next step: to help invent and actively create a future that generates exceptional value.

It has been argued that companies have to excel at three things simultaneously:

1. Letting go of the past
2. Improving the present and
3. Creating the future

Of these three, companies are best at the middle element. The urgencies of quarterly results mean that performance management gets primary attention. When you have to answer to the market with such frequency, then whatever is impeding today's results has to be dealt with immediately.

Alas, done precipitously, we often soar today, undermine our long-term competitiveness, and plunge as dramatically tomorrow. (We will talk about the first factor—letting go of the past—in a minute.)

Here's an example. Omar worked with a key client who exhibited this short-term focus to the extreme. To make their end of year numbers, the sales director flooded the company's distributors with their products. Using their corporate clout, the distributors were muscled into accepting the products even though the quantities were far in excess of current market demand or what the distributors wanted for stock purposes.

On the client's balance sheet this produced the appearance of tremendous sales results, product movement, and progress. Alas, as soon as the next calendar and financial year dawned, the market was saturated with their products; distributors revolted, and like a house of cards the whole edifice built on numerous quarters of this type of legerdemain, came tumbling down.

It then took a full year of bitter medicine and fierce internal confrontations that Sensei had to adjudicate and facilitate. Everyone blamed everyone else for the debacle alleging either malfeasance or at least nonfeasance. The sales director vehemently denied that anything was fundamentally amiss at all. At the end, they had to take a hit for three quarters running, remove the sales director and rehabilitate their relationships with their distributors before the company returned to profitable sales-led growth.

Despite examples such as this, of the three factors companies are best at, performance management gets the greatest attention. But in doing so, today's stars often miss tomorrow's opportunities because of yesterday's blinders.

We are not arguing for forgetting a company's legacy, or founding values, or those intrinsic aspects of its culture or vision that give it vitality and purpose. For example, Isadore Sharp, the founder of The Four Seasons Hotel chain, has built his luxury hotel brand on a premise of utter dedication to client needs without undue frills. His formula has involved hiring the best people and asking them to do what is needed to satisfy the guests. Do what you would want done for yourself to make guests comfortable is the company's charge. Their dedication to enveloping the customer in warm, elegant, encompassing hospitality that unobtrusively delights the senses, soothes as well as stimulates—each in their own turn (depending for example whether you are at one of their award-winning spas or restaurants)—is not something they can afford to let go of. Accordingly, the Four Seasons doesn't have multiple brands and they are utterly focused on their target niche.

So we fully agree that we must hang on, even devotionally at times, to founding principles like Johnson & Johnson's legendary credo which calls first for improving the lives of those doctors and nurses, fathers and mothers; all those who use their products; and then the lives of its employees, the communities in which they operate, and *finally* the stockholders (who they argue will get a fair return if these other principles are fully delivered). Such defining statements are sacrosanct, and are sources of enormous passion and pride.

On the other hand, the past is also the source of many chains, not just life-giving roots. And these chains must be identified and broken. In fact, one of the primary jobs of leaders must be to help the organization *separate out the roots from the chains*.

The chains can include outmoded structures that include:

- overly diffuse supply chain structures begging to be rationalized so that the same activities aren't being duplicated around the world;

- Byzantine processes which need multiple approval or sign-offs to get decisions made or customer requests processed;

- addiction to past technology shown by the mainframe fascination at IBM, or the aversion to digital technology at Kodak;

- stodgy inbreeding of leadership of the type many large companies so often suffocate on before bringing in CEOs from outside as a "cure";

- misapplied methodologies as seen both at Home Depot and 3M where the new leaders thought that the greater efficiency produced by Six Sigma—experienced by them at GE—would be a transformational panacea. Only after time did it become evident that at Home Depot this led to the erosion of customer-intimacy and at 3M to a dissipation of their innovative fervor;

- basking in past superiority shown by banks initially ignoring other providers of credit and leasing as these "disruptors" virtually decimated one of their profit centers.

How do we break the chains? By having a powerful and compelling future articulated and advanced.

Easier said than done of course. So the first mental step is to agree that certain past preferences (i.e. the chains) are not intrinsic to our organization's identity, but were tools, or strategies, or methodologies that worked admirably at a certain time for a certain purpose. However, they now must be amended, recreated, or perhaps even scrapped.

Then, once we are mentally clear on the roots that we must continue to nourish to ensure our company's success, we have to envision a future powerful enough such that we are almost obliged to divest ourselves of the chains that are holding us back. Only then are we emotionally and paradigmatically liberated so as to be able to provoke and perhaps even augur in the future.

In what follows, we will show you a number of ways that this can be pragmatically accomplished.

Self-cannibalization

One of the most interesting approaches for creating the conditions that will allow such a powerful future to be invented and to sever our past chains is simply to create a team within the organization whose job is to antiquate our own current best product, service, or value experience before the competition does.

If you stop and think about that for a second, you will see it makes wonderful sense. If we are serious contenders in the marketplace, and come up with a market winner, all our competitors will devote their time to one thing: usurping our leadership position or whittling down our lead.

While it is important to defend and to continue to improve quality, and communicate the value proposition in a way that cements our superiority in the minds and hearts of consumers, more is needed.

If we can top our own best (rather than fall in love with it) before someone else does, we will continue to be or at least *lead* the leading edge.

During its heyday, Gillette excelled at this. As they released a new blade, say the Aftra, teams would be set up whose job was to beat this blade and invent the next generation (the Mach 3) before anyone else did. With the Walkman, Sony did the very same thing. They continually found improvements (from size reduction, to adding Dolby and auto-reverse) and came to market with them, just as their competitors were just "matching" their last model.

It is fascinating that today's breakthroughs can become tomorrow's chains. Sony almost assiduously refused to see the emerging possibility of the iPod (now allowing music, not just the ability to play it, to be portable), and even the iPhone (combining technologies that Sony has arguably excelled at), though both are natural successors to the Walkman.

But notice what we are counseling. The need is not just to improve our products. Everyone does that as a matter of course. What we are saying is that you want to create a new product that makes your existing one obsolete.

And here more than self-cannibalization teams may be needed, particularly if the market opportunity is not a new generation of your product, but a re-imagining of that value dimension or potentiality. That may require a whole new corporate DNA.

Clayton Christensen sketched this quandary brilliantly in his book *The Innovator's Dilemma*. His central argument is that when a disruptive technology is first glimpsed by the market, it is unwieldy and possibly suboptimal, and so doesn't attract avid activists from among those companies for whom it would be a natural fit.

After all, it would be hard to make an argument to a management board to divert funds from currently successful products and services to those that would cost more, earn less, and dissatisfy the current customer base. Imagine having asked, at the time PCs were just emerging, computer makers earning a $200,000 profit per sale on industrial size computers to shift to an erratic, plodding PC where they might make $2,000 per sale while damaging their current brand and technology standing. On the face of it, you are likely to be laughed out of the room.

As a result of these forces and pressures, established firms continue to do business as they always have.

However, as these firms continue along, someone experiments with the new technology, improves it, attracts new customers for it (for example, current non-users of the existing technology), and/or lures those who are happy to have broader options (for example portability in the computer example, even though at this point the product is not quite as good as it is going to get). Then, drawing on this new and growing fan base, these new innovators naturally work out the past kinks and deficits and approximate in time and even exceed the capacity of what the incumbents can offer.

Before we know it, we have moved from typewriters to word processors, from mainframes to PCs, from faxes to the internet; from only banks issuing credit cards to bookstores and airlines and gas stations issuing credit cards; from express mail to overnight couriers to scanned documents, and more.

If this is the historical pattern, why don't entrenched companies do something about it? The answer is that it is very hard to jettison what is currently working—particularly due to the short-term market realities we mentioned before.

Therefore we almost have to create a separate division, or profit and loss center, whose job it is to explore new, disruptive ideas; look for ways to make them profitable, and launch prototypes before new or existing competitors steal a march on us.

So, as a passion liberator, self-cannibalization works where we are seeking to trounce our own leadership before someone else does. We can be excited and passionate to be paving the next step; to be part of teams who seek to constantly beat our best; to ask the unaskable questions; to be people who listen for the most pressing and recurring frustrations expressed by fans, cynics, *and* overall users.

But when a particular challenge to our very operating model surfaces, we may have to hive off a division or business unit that takes a really deep dive into the challenge. This requires us to understand the possible profit structure needed, the type of people that have to be recruited, the marketing and R&D involved, and the potential application of this new technology and approach.

After listening to Omar talk about this at a conference, a vice president of Intel told us: "You're quite right. We're Intel, we're a really smart company, and virtually every computer has a label saying 'Intel inside.' But we missed the internet revolution! We had young kids in our company surfing the net, and instead of studying the phenomenon we told them to get focused and get serious! It was under our noses. And when they tried to tell us, we wouldn't listen."

When we are out of step with where the world, or at least our world, is moving, it kills not only passion, but possibility. And invariably senior management is the biggest offender being custodians of the past. As a result, they are usually the most reluctant to change.

To be fair, what is passé was likely "revolutionary" when it was moving up through the ranks. Senior management may have made their careers on it. It is hard to relinquish what you believe you owe your success to. When it has been so much to you, it becomes not only then a time-bound solution, one among many, but almost a personal talisman.

A leading transportation company that Sensei has assisted has a legendary leader who, for 40 years, has dominated the industry. He grew up at a time when the company took over the industry through a strict operating excellence model— highly process driven, assuring efficiency, and finding customers who were very pliant as long as this was assured. That company is today tottering with billion dollar losses. Their customers are opting for multiple solutions through multiple providers, "cherry picking" and customizing a suite of solutions to meet their transport needs. Refusing to acknowledge there is another way, even the operational excellence at this once proud company has slipped precipitously.

It is a company with a remarkably robust brand. However, renaissance will only occur if the infatuation with a past inflexible operating model is revised, and "transport" and "logistics" are looked at with radically new eyes.

Therefore, business leaders must always meticulously explore or research alternatives: show either how changes and innovations can help better fulfill the potential of the current winning products or services; or show how what once made this current model or approach or solution so much of a breakthrough is going to become a liability.

A critical way to protect and unleash fresh passion to co-create an exciting future can be done by creating specific teams or units that are authorized and mandated to seek out such stimuli, to sniff out such opportunities, and be rewarded for bringing them up constructively and viably.

Where should such teams seek information to determine what current products need to be radically improved (or made obsolete)? They should consult the marketplace as well as fringe competitors who are gobbling up niches; industry-leading suppliers who can suggest where the overall value chain may be heading; and even the gripes and exasperations of the company's most talented employees (who tend to know when the company is missing the boat).

But make the relaying of such thoughts, ideas, explorations, options and opportunities something that is honored, recognized, and respected virtually above all else. As Plato pointed out so long ago, "What is honored in a country will be cultivated there." So, too, in a company.

Once such ideas and impetus are on hand, we are ready to provoke the future. Our only other option is to remain mired in an increasingly unprofitable past.

The Provocative Future

To apply this tool requires that the right bull's eye be in place. As we hunt for potential sources of fresh value and competitive advantage, our search is bounded by the following. As we've said, we are looking specifically to create a world where our passions and talents intersect, and where we are focusing our energies in areas where substantially deep profit pools currently or potentially exist.

The "provocative future" is important because it will show us the next step to take.

The way to apply the provocative future is to, as we've suggested, take a look at the most pressing challenges that are keeping us stuck, or the things that grate most on our customers and clients, or those things that are most exciting on various relevant horizons.

Having taken a clear look at these, we then describe an audacious future in which the problems are either gone, or transcended, or transformed; or the opportunities realized or reeled in.

Having stated this breakthrough future state, we then *brainstorm backwards* from that future to today.

So, for example, when Diner's Club invented the first widely used credit card (given their current status in the market, the only thought that comes to mind is "oh, how the mighty have fallen"), their provocative future statement was something akin to: "We will make it so that customers will not need cash to go out to dinner."

Back then (the 1940s) this would have sounded outlandish. But locating a way that people could dine without worrying about cash in hand changed the way we all not only dine, but consume and to some extent, live.

Another example cited by future-provoking creativity mavens like the incomparable Edward de Bono, who has done more to educate us about practical thinking and creativity than virtually anyone, is the Olympics. The profit model of the Olympics was originally based on audience attendance or as our U.K. colleagues might put it "bums on seats." The Olympics continued to lose money solidly on this basis.

They restated their provocative future into something like: "We will make money even if no one attends." And shifting their profit model to television rights and promotional benefit has transformed the Olympics into not only a huge profit generator but such a symbol of prestige that cities all over the world vie, in a state of acute frenzy, to host it.

It takes real insight to locate and state a truly future-eliciting provocative future. So, that your phone will be a communication and entertainment center is an example here. For iPod, when it was conceived, a core insight would have been, you'll always have your favorite music with you—at the beach, on a mountaintop, anywhere. You won't have to "select" what to take.

Once a provocative future that solves a pressing current problem, or combines multiple customer values and desires, is expressed, you cannot ask "*if*" it's possible. This tool only works if you assume it WILL happen. Only then can we construct a bridge from that future to today—if necessary, milestone by milestone.

Sometimes a fully stated provocative future will deliver outrageous value even if it falls somewhat short of the full audacious aspiration expressed. For example, when facilitating large groups Omar often grappled with the challenge of how to get people back in time after breaks, particularly on multi-day learning experiences, packed with multiple sessions, when time was of the essence.

The provocative future Sensei stated was: "Participants will WANT to arrive on time." Then imagining participants rushing to get back into the conference room, it was a matter of asking: "What would make this true?"

There are punitive measures like having to make a financial donation for tardiness, but these get too somber. So instead, Omar created a system where the first time someone was late, he/she sang a song. The second time, he got a chance to dance for the group. The third time, it was the audience's choice. Omar and his team were also liable if they were late. It was truly done with a very light sense of humor. Pretty soon, people began racing back to make sure that they were not the last one back.

No, at first not everyone made it back on time. But after the first public song, people were frantically heading back.

You have to act as if the future you want to create *has* happened. And even if you don't fully succeed in fact, you will have gotten much farther than if you had merely stated iterative, tentative goals that really aren't much of a stretch to achieve.

This Works Everywhere

The provocative future works for all kinds of industries. Consider the training profession. Often money is poured into training with scant consideration of real ROI or organizational value. There is a vain hope it must be doing some good in most organizations.

What if organizations and training companies stated the following provocative future? "Each hour of training will contribute tangibly to our company's success."

Then the whole training process would be designed to deliver against that goal. That would mean clear priorities would be established and specific agendas set. It's shameful how few people attending a training session even know the purpose of their attendance other than some vague statement about "building skills" that will rarely ever be tracked once the session is over. It would mean follow-up requiring accountability for solid application agreed and done. Finally, we would measure the contribution made to the strategic goals or tactical imperatives the training was meant to serve.

As you can see from the above description, this would be far more energy intensive. We would do fewer sessions, invest more in them, and demand more from deliverers, attendees, and bosses. And most critically, we could track and measure results, ensuring ROI just as in every other corporate activity.

At the other end of the spectrum, large conventional consulting firms provide elaborate models, frameworks, reams of statistics, often ponderous analysis, and a lengthy exposition of recommendations. Wouldn't it be nice if all consultants chose a provocative future similar to: "Clients will take real action to implement our recommendations."

If they did, even the largest consulting firms would shift their considerable talents to client engagement and true partnering, standing alongside their clients as they initially bring the recommendations online.

Most anti-consultant sentiment stems from their academic advice or accusations of their never dealing with real-world applications. Moving forward, consulting solutions and agreements should include metrics related to execution and not just the publishing of untested hypotheses.

You can transform your company, your niche, and your industry by selecting a provocative future that taps the greatest yearnings and some of the unfulfilled hopes of the people you serve. And this must be a future compelling enough—one that serves as a key must-win battle you've established (See Passion Liberator Two: The Right Bull's Eye) and lays essential groundwork for your ultimate visionary purpose.

Provocative futures can be used throughout the organization in order to address all kinds of challenges. One of Sensei's clients operating in Vietnam struggled with retaining top employees. They were one of the early movers in that market and attracted and groomed some of the most promising local talent. As Vietnam continued to grow by leaps and bounds, new entrants had sought to poach from this company. Clearly their strategy could not be to keep raising salaries. New entrants to the market will always benchmark the salary paid by the market leader and beat that, in order to attract the most talented people.

The company realized it would have to take aim at a different provocative future: "We will be the best choice for the best talent and they will be proud as Vietnamese to work with us."

Just hearing the statement, you can just imagine the type of leadership energy, the nurturing of careers and talent, the providing of exposure to challenges and opportunities, the commitment to the country and the developing communities within Vietnam that would be required for this to be more than a hollow slogan.

But as in the example above, once stated, what will be required is often very evident. Leadership is then expressed in taking action *today* to make that future more real each and every day. And as long as this is the gauntlet we first accept ourselves and then throw down for our teams, passion will never be far away.

For this company in Vietnam, in order for this provocative future to become real, groups across the organization had to be tapped to generate the range of ideas required for making this so. With those ideas in hand, generated from across the organization, they are in the midst of making a true effort to make this commitment real. As of this writing, turnover is down, retention is up, and the employees are part of an ongoing task force dedicated to bringing this provocative future to life, increasingly each day.

The Shared Results Conversation

We can also provoke the future by catalyzing creative, purposeful, focused action, team by team, individual by individual. Here's how.

While we will give an example of applying this tool to individuals, everything we say here would also apply equally and naturally to teams. There we would use the team as a "unit" and replicate the conversation we are recommending for individuals.

Let's first start with the instance of when you are the boss. You approach a direct report and say: "Looking ahead six months, here are the three most important things that, if you did, would absolutely *Wow* me."

This works if the three things are both fundamental enough and adaptive enough to evoke and provoke the person's best. By "fundamental" we mean clearly tied to the largest aims of your organization, or business unit, or department. By "adaptive" we mean requiring personal growth and initiative.

So a good "*Wow*" would *not* be, "You would *Wow* me if you sold 100 more widgets." This is a simple KPI (key performance indicator) and doesn't need reaffirmation. A good *Wow* would be, "You would *Wow* me if you brought in 10 new profitable clients, and helped us recover five dormant ones. That's central to our sales and customer connection strategy and is different from our current approach of churn and burn."

Again, it would not be very helpful to say: "You would *Wow* me if all your people filled in their performance development paperwork." It would be by comparison scintillating to state: "You would *Wow* me if your team fully engaged in the performance development process; if we saw real coaching dialogues take place during the reviews that result in powerful future-creating action plans we could monitor and encourage."

So you share your highest impact top three *Wow*s with each direct report. Why three? Psychological research suggests a rule of three in human focus and attention. Any more than three, and attention wanders and focus gets scattered. Moreover, Sensei's global work with leadership teams suggests strongly that virtually everyone *has* three to four top "satisfaction" conditions for his/her team members, consciously or otherwise. But thinking about them consciously forces us to clarify and articulate them, and most critically to *share* them while the person can still do something about them.

After the *Wow*s have been shared, ask your team mates to take a few days to write in their own words, what they have understood. Schedule a brief appointment to review that, as well as to hear from them what they *will need from you* in terms of leadership support, mentoring, and coaching to make this provocative future happen. This becomes a mutual coaching contract.

Then agree to the regularity and mode of check-ins. We recommend a minimum of a monthly "health check" (similar to the radical conversations) and a maximum of a fortnightly update.

Now you can work this in the opposite direction too, and you should. Ask your boss. Say you need just five minutes to get some help to better deliver your goals. It's a hard request to say "no" to, given the time you've asked for and the rationale you've stated.

When you meet simply say: "Boss, I have a good understanding of the goals we've sketched. But I want to be absolutely clear on your and our priorities. Suppose its six months (or three or nine, depending on the nature of your work, industry and interaction) hence. And you are absolutely overjoyed by my membership on your team and the contribution I've made. What are the three most critical achievements that would make that true?"

If your boss says, "I'll have to think about that," agree to a follow-up of five minutes face-to-face or via telecom at any time within two weeks (ideally) so it stays fresh.

If your boss gives you an overly technical *Wow* (improve our margins in product "x"), simply expand it by asking, "And as a result the type of action and behavior and follow-up you're expecting is…" Then offer your own hypothesis for the boss to either corroborate or amend.

After the exchange, drop a brief note with your understanding of the three biggest *Wow* factors identified. After about a month, ask the boss, "How am I doing?" Hopefully with some demonstrated progress, you will motivate them to respond positively when you then request that a quick monthly feedback become a regular feature, and perhaps even make a request or two of what you might want or need from your boss to deliver on these priorities.

Why ask your boss? Because it is very likely your boss already *has* three (or so) most critical "success factors" that tower above all the other objectives she has for you. You might as well find out what they are and heighten your boss's appreciation of your progress in this regard. Your boss in this way can be enrolled as your coaching and achievement partner.

If someone refuses to have such a dialogue with you, essentially they are indicating that they aren't serious about the relationship or its future. While initially disheartening, it will at least give you a realistic sense of where you stand and how you may need to manage or move on.

But set up properly, as a win-win and stated as helping to achieve their own priorities, very few bosses will be so ludicrously apathetic or disengaged as to swat away such zeal and commitment.

The shared results conversation can be applied in all kinds of context, not just with direct reports or bosses. It can and should be applied to constructively provoke the future *any time you have to produce a shared result with someone else.*

So, for example, with a potential new client or customer, you might begin this way: "Say you make the decision to work with us. It's six months hence. What are the three most critical things you would need from us for you to feel this was the best possible decision you could have made?"

As you hear their replies you can assess how well you can respond to these expectations. You might and may want to fine-tune your organization's responsiveness accordingly.

But if their desires are out of synch with your abilities, you can either save both parties significant aggravation by suggesting that you are not right for them (remember we have to be true to our visionary purpose and values), or you could educate the client in terms of how you *can* meet their needs and what they can realistically expect and the extent to which you can truly *Wow* them. Then follow-up regularly to ensure the *Wow* is being produced.

If you do this you will have a lifelong fan and advocate as a result.

Moreover, once you've started coming through for them, you might even let them know how reciprocally they could get better terms, command premium attention, among others. If a client knows what paperwork to pre-fill to get expedited attention, or how paying invoices earlier will allow them better rates, then they will often be inspired to create a truly thriving partnership with you. This way we provoke the business-building relationships we want to have.

As we can see, this same conversation can happen with suppliers, colleagues, within project teams, across the entire range of corporate interaction. In fact, coupled with the "possibility focus" (see Chapter 7, Passion Liberator Four: Protecting Possibility), this becomes an exceptional way to ensure that forward momentum remains as charged and as dynamic as we would like it to be.

In fact, try it at home too. Before starting a new year with your spouse and family, before embarking on a vacation, look ahead and imagine it has been the best "X" (year, vacation, sex, whatever) ever. Then ask what would actually make it so for the other person or people. Also share with them what would make that true for you. Aligning your *Wows* will produce powerful, perhaps even radical dialogues, as well as ramp up the passion and greatly optimize your time together.

Remember, whether you elicit it from them or not, your loved ones almost certainly *have* these desires and hopes. Why hide from them? Equally, we almost certainly have our own peeves and wishes. The better we understand theirs and the better they understand ours, the more rewarding and energizing our interactions can be.

Putting This to Work

To apply this passion liberator, realize we have to balance breaking free of the past with inventing the future.

Our first act as leaders, wherever we operate, is to separate our "roots" from our "chains." And we have to break the chains by creating future-focused alternatives to them.

We can do this by self-cannibalizing our current best; by checking-in with people with different perspectives; by running numerous scenarios informed by research and interaction with people both inside and outside (suppliers, customers, etc.) the company.

And we can do this by creating a "skunks works" team, one that is immunized from the daily corporate exigencies, assumptions, and pressures.

Also, wherever we are stuck, wherever we feel more is possible, wherever we are at a seeming plateau, state a reality-altering provocative future. Then ask, "What else would have to change for this to be true?" And each day let's show up ready to exemplify the "what else."

And then with a wide cross-section of people, let's brainstorm backwards to today, creating a results path to this future and acknowledge, recognize, and reward all action that takes us there.

Finally, let's make the present *and* future more vibrant by having shared results conversations that forge new relationships, further current ones, and help us to make manifest, abundant new aligned possibilities.

CHAPTER 9

PASSION LIBERATOR SIX: CLAIMING ACCOUNTABILITY

Exciting as it is to have a provocative, possibility-rich future before us, in order to make it real, leaders, team members, contributors at all levels have to claim accountability. In fact, being detached from accountability is one of the greatest passion killers.

By accountability we mean understanding WHAT must be done, WHY it must happen and HOW I can make it so.

To be more specific, in leadership terms what kind of accountability has to be claimed? There is a generic accountability of course, namely to ask tirelessly: "What can *I* do about this (specific situation)?"

You would think that would be a given, but it is not. We have worked with literally hundreds of clients and after they have explained in detail why they have called to ask for our help, virtually no one says, "I've done everything that is possible to do. I have accepted all the accountability I can, displayed all the proactivity I can, and I am truly spent."

Far more often, we hear the resigned sighs of those who report what they "would" have done if there hadn't been some (always external to them of course) impediment. They tell us they didn't have enough time, they have a lousy boss, or mulish employees.

They (and we) employ these and a host of other dodges, to deliver us from the accountability of taking all the action we sensibly can to make a difference.

Lamentably, taking ourselves off the hook, while temporarily easier, sucks vitality and engagement from us. It is a primary way of deadening passion. Those who *do* take such action seem remarkable, heroic, and extraordinary. Actually it is probably the quintessence of leadership—a "can do" determination that translates into results. And the more we radiate this as leaders and exemplify this and inspire this in our teams, the more passion is naturally released organization-wide as we are all then busy advancing the frontiers of what is possible. Passion and engagement almost inextricably accompany each other.

While it might seem on the surface that the choice we face is to take ownership of the situation or not, the fundamental choice we face is even more searing and existential. We either choose to be a victim—or not.

And if we choose not, if we choose to move our world forward rather than to whine about its challenges, then we will always look for what we *can* influence or progress, whether it be infinitesimal or exceptional. We've spoken about this to a large extent already.

But claiming accountability in terms of leadership has an even more seminal focus and application. Namely, it is about holding yourself accountable for getting the very best from people: from bosses, colleagues across functions, direct reports and more. If indeed, success comes from successful relationships, this is very crucially the case.

So in fleshing out this passion liberator we will take a two-pronged view. We'll first look at two key tools for claiming personal and collective accountability in dealing with external challenges and opportunities once a provocative future has been stated.

Then, we will look at how we can be optimally accountable and "response-able" in enrolling the best from those we work with. Not only will doing so liberate our own passion, but done properly, it will liberate theirs as well.

Taking on Problems and Harvesting Opportunities

Sometimes there is a problem we don't quite know how to solve. Either it seems genuinely insoluble or it has been in place for so long that there is institutional inertia relative to taking it on.

When it seems there is no way forward to the provocative future you have stated, and all the evident ways to deal with it have either failed or been counterproductive, the best tool we've encountered for moving forward is called a "deep dive."

As articulated by leaders at GE, Microsoft, HP and elsewhere, it consists of immersing ourselves deeply in a problem without rushing to resolve it. It means living with it, and interacting with people who own aspects of it, or who can provide insight into obstacles or even solutions relative to it.

During this time, as ever, keep a mindset of "wonder" and "curiosity," and insist on fully appreciating what is. And the experience of the companies that have deployed this almost Zen-like practice, is that in time, when there are no pre-set assumptions about what it will take to solve the problem, and enough openness, enough listening, enough exploration, enough unromantic fact-gathering have taken place, a way presents itself.

Here's an example. Sensei worked with a major transportation and logistics company that had achieved breakthrough results in a developing market through inspired leadership and by building a highly impressive local team. They had managed to completely turn around a deeply troubled division, making it one of the company's brightest lights in the process.

But after several years of outstanding results had been posted, discontent among employees, who believed they were being substantially underpaid, started to grow. They realized their industry didn't typically pay as well as others, but they thought that was a massive cop-out. They knew they were employed by a global leader who earned large profits. And they understood that delivering the excellence they did in a developing country with challenging norms relative to customs, transport hubs, ports, containerization, IT, infrastructure, was more difficult, not less. They wanted pay commensurate with their talent, the results they were producing, and in line with what top executives commanded at the best companies in their field.

Rationally, in a talent-led era, in an allegedly meritocratic organization, it was hard to argue against them. However, this had been considered a mine-field for years. Conventional wisdom from the European head office was that a professionally conducted salary survey would show the pay package was "competitive." Given that, the head office claimed that their reluctance came from the fact that the survey would only confirm they were paying fairly and they feared that revealing the company's pay scale to everyone (which if the survey were made public would happen) would just create animus and unhelpful rivalry and hurt overall morale.

Getting to the Heart of Problem Solving

The current head of the unhappy division, Jean-Marc, told his bosses he felt this argument against raising pay didn't hold water. If his team were "adult" enough to deal with the stresses and challenges of delivering superior results in the difficult situations they faced daily, perhaps they could be trusted to know the truth about who was paid what. Moreover, gossip circulated anyway about pay packages, so it would be better for people to know rather than to erroneously suppose.

Moreover, Jean-Marc insisted that if the rationale for the pay scale and for bonuses and other rewards was indeed rationally meritocratic, then it would be simply a matter of leaders like him explaining to their people why objectively some contributors should be paid more.

Jean-Marc told his bosses that he would lose the trust of a team that had delivered so much for the company if they didn't have the survey done. It would also seem as if the company had something to hide. Once the results were in, if indeed the pay *was* competitive, *hallelujah*! If as everyone suspected, it wasn't, then it would take more than dogmatic assertions to deal with it.

Jean-Marc put together a team and they did a deep dive. They visited other companies. They looked at open-book accounting whereby employees know the profit and loss specifics of the company and so understand the rationale, relevance and importance of various decisions and options. They considered this and all other options that they came across. They also visited their European bosses, and heard out their concerns.

And when the results of the salary survey showed indeed that the employees were underpaid, Jean-Marc, based on the immersion, had already engineered a staged redress that protected budgets for the current year. The redress also allowed the new system to come fully online in the succeeding year, where the company profit growth more than allowed for the increases without jeopardizing the plans they had committed to.

The team knew they had to help him "sell" it. They truly rallied and stretched to ensure that no one could rationally say the organization was going to suffer in order to do justice to its people. Production and profitability, both already high, increased further.

Moreover, Jean-Marc demonstrated the real costs of losing the stars who were otherwise shopping their CVs, and the potential impact of the company's inability to recruit for key positions given the unacceptable package they were able to offer earlier. He demonstrated that the potential impact annually would be more than twice the increase being sought, certainly in the next several years if they lost more and more top performers and were unable to bring in stellar people for key roles.

He was able to put together a solution, because he took full accountability for solving a problem that everyone else had given up on, given all the politics and all the stakeholders involved. Having taken a public stand, he was passionate about finding a way.

Essentially Jean-Marc pulled it off by almost "recruiting" key bosses, team members, and other industry allies, until they came to feel it was their bull's eye as well. He linked this crusade to their viability as a company who would or would not have the leaders needed to continue to deliver the growth they had. This therefore became a large-scale Manhattan Project as we have spoken of previously. The employees didn't continue to malinger with petty gripes or argue minutiae. They realized it was in everyone's best interest. Therefore to be flexible, they would all have to defer to the facts as they were discovered, and then give the company time to make this possible.

There was a resultant gusher of enthusiasm and excitement as this was resolved and people's pay packages went up. Key people re-dedicated themselves to the company and the new system became a global example for the parent company in terms of fairness and transparency. And alongside all this, the company was able to attract the critically needed new talent given the continued growth.

Jean-Marc had forced everyone to "live with the problem" long enough for a solution to almost just *emerge*. (For more on this process see Chapter 11 and the discussion on communicating in a way that releases potential.) It emerged as bickering faded into the background and a joint dedication to making the solution workable took its place.

Let's underscore what happened here. When you use this tool, you need to clearly state both the problem *and* the opportunity. Then identify the major stakeholders and see how many of them you can enroll by finding an aspect of this opportunity that links up with things they acknowledge to be critical. In this case it was the continued cost-effective viability of supporting and continuing to enable this company's growth. Then, without rushing to devise a solution, spend time interviewing, interacting, questioning, exploring, in concert with a myriad of internal, and if necessary, external resources.

As a solution seems to emerge from all this interaction, fine-tune and shape it with a variety of people, looking at its pluses and minuses. And don't prematurely fall in love with a solution. The trick is always to ask of an idea that we are rapidly growing infatuated with, "How can we make this good idea *better*?"

Art of Rapid Prototyping

This point leads us to the second "tool." The commitment to continuous improvement should emphatically *not* be taken as a counsel to inaction *until* the idea is in "ideal" shape.

The second tool for claiming accountability in transforming challenges into robust opportunities is rapid prototyping. The premise is that you *rapidly* cobble together a workable approximate of what you'd ultimately like; get massive and widespread feedback; tinker some more, gather more input; and thereby generate something that is truly fit for your purpose.

The alternative is to keep fine-tuning endlessly, and purely internally. Internal here can mean your own department, team, business unit, or indeed the organization. Then, deeply invested in the result on which you've labored so mightily for so long, you expose it to others.

If you take that approach, you have two potential problems as we highlighted at the outset.

First, if what you've produced (be it an ad campaign, product packaging, a process redesign, a supply chain manifesto, a new product mix, a new office layout suggestion, whatever), violates the hopes, or expectations, or biases of other key stakeholders (your boss, another department head, a business partner, customer, consumer group), they will feel threatened by its seeming imminence, by the fact that it seems almost "done."

Psychologically, when we are presented with what even *seems* like a *fait accompli*, and we are uncomfortable with it, we galvanize ourselves for massive resistance.

Therefore rather than getting people's helpful "recommendations," when presenting at this late stage we are likely to hear entrenched emotional positions if anything seems at all awry to anyone. Moreover, not having been consulted earlier, some stakeholders may feel blindsided and shocked that you would have taken something this far without getting their earlier buy-in and endorsement. They will drag their heels at best when presented with what you have.

Psychologically at your own end, a different, equally pernicious factor will be at work. Precisely because you have developed this over such a long period of time, precisely because you have studied it, revised it, sought to improve it before exposing it to anyone else, you will see all the strengths of the ideas, and be potentially dismissive of the downsides. You are likely to respond with equal hostility to the challenges and may even be unhealthily territorial and proprietary relative to the proposal.

Instead of collective energies being pooled towards making this idea happen, those presenting and those being presented to will become mutual passion killers for each other.

The alternative is the rapid prototyping paradigm. Ad agencies know the premise for this well. In this field, it is natural to throw lots of ideas out, live with the best ones (the deep dive described above); try to intuit what feelings we want to engender in the consumer; look at it literally, drift laterally; and wait for the muse to whisper in our ear. We can imagine the quintessential simplicity that is sought for and which at the best of time emerges. Consider the relatively hallowed (in terms of ad campaigns anyway) example from the past, when after months of monastic silence, some of the brightest minds in communication working on behalf of Coke emerged with "Coke is it."

Imagine all the discarded portentous and unwieldy verbal persiflage that must have (metaphorically) been on the cutting room floor, for this ray of communication clarity to emerge.

That is the aim essentially of both the deep dive and rapid prototyping. Of course the first need is always to make sure we understand what we are innovating on behalf of and what a real solution would have to contain and deliver. Otherwise we will, to use a less hallowed Coke example, end up with "New Coke."

The second need is to get us out of the procrastination trap, which also leeches energy and passion. The procrastination trap is fueled by our desire to not embark on something until it is "right." Prototyping says, get something, almost anything, out quickly. Approximate what you cannot immediately perhaps fully conceive or achieve. But then, let it go for a bit, get away from it, get feedback from potential users, bystanders, experts, renegades.

And it's much easier when they're providing input at a time when they can influence direction. You have no real investment in the final design or solution yet. However you are at least providing a context for the views, a template for them to improve. You're not relinquishing accountability; you're wielding it in a way that builds up communication, relationships, and possibility.

The act of embarking on rapid prototyping unleashes passion, because it is edgy, emphatic, urgent, high tempo, buzzing with views and reviews; and because each bout of prototyping involves reviewing the original purpose and blending our own ideas with massive external stimulus.

Many times the examples given on behalf of prototyping refer to august teams from the past, for example, Sid Caesar's remarkable comedy writing team that included talents like Neil Simon, Woody Allen, Mel Brooks, Larry Gelbart, and more. They produced weekly comedy shows, and ideas were churned, challenged, improved, and improvised from there. Show segments were constantly being prototyped.

The most famous example of rapid prototyping is the actual Manhattan Project, where the world's leading scientists were corralled together, and then charged with an overarching aim— to beat Germany to the bomb.

No one knew what the solution was or would turn out to be. What induced the result was massive prototyping following promising trails and frequent blind trails; constantly checking and rechecking against results; bouncing off ideas; and embracing and challenging instinct concurrently.

However, rapid prototyping is not only for moments like these, where something utterly new has to be conceived or invented. Any improvement, any key report, any major communication, any organizational redesign, would benefit from this approach of having initial ideas subjected to the crucible of wide-scale involvement. And after more feedback, engendering further innovation, what emerges is something sculpted from generative, wide-scale, passionate engagement.

Concurrent development, rather than sequential development of ideas and ways forward, has to be the approach. That is the only way that true dialogue can occur, real passion liberated and real collective potential realized.

The Boss Dimension to Accountability

Let's move now to the people dimension of engagement and accountability.

The first arena, in which we have to claim accountability, in order to be custodians of both our results and our passion, is in our interaction with our boss. This is the person to whom we are ultimately accountable for the results we produce.

Two approaches apply here: the first is to liberate or perhaps even nurture passion in your boss (a seemingly odd conception that we'll explore); the second is a way to protect your own passion as you deal with the vicissitudes of behavior that you may encounter with a variety of bosses, some who may have a style that grates with your own.

The first bit of clarity we need relative to bosses is to avoid finding ourselves in an inherent parent-child relationship in which we are the whiny child petitioning for scraps of approval, approbation, attention, interest, and validation.

One way to "level the playing field" is by figuring ways to motivate your boss.

We always hear about how bosses should motivate those who report to them. But in the bulging literature on leadership, management, and coaching, you rarely come across any insights on *motivating your boss in turn*.

Why is that? Why is it assumed that someone in a hierarchically superior position loses all the need for motivation, feedback, approval, interest, and more?

Perhaps it is assumed that a direct report can't supply it—that the only source it can come from is "above." But that's ridiculous! The prime audience we all have is our teams. And while we actively *need* emotional acclaim, perhaps due to job security, advancement and other concerns from our boss, as human beings we need it from those we engage at all levels almost as much.

So let's make our peace with the fact that bosses are human. As such, whether they show it or not, they are often confused, unsure, uncertain, and when they get it right, it is in our best interests to let them know it. This is not only to buoy them, but to help them craft a winning leadership game sheet. Otherwise they are likely to do whatever is "easier" or more "natural" to them, irrespective of the emotional impact on others (read: you).

And by doing this, you can indirectly, and non-threateningly, give your bosses feedback about what they are doing that *doesn't* work as well.

One of Omar's clients was the Asia director of a major consumer goods conglomerate. His boss was overbearing, bombastic, and almost assiduously insensitive.

Omar's client, Paul, was railing at the counterproductive visits of his boss, Frank. In the wake of these visits, Paul had to put the team back together, salve wounded pride, and resurrect a sense of willingness, and purpose as well.

"Can you believe it?" asked Paul. "One of our most senior leaders is an expert at decimating passion, morale, and commitment."

Omar asked him if Frank had ever conducted a visit that hadn't been such an unmitigated disaster. Looking thoughtful, Paul admitted he had.

"Funny you should ask," began Paul, "just last week his visit to Thailand was a dream. Maybe he had a good week at home, hell I don't know. But he was relaxed, positive, he listened, he even gave the odd encouraging comment. The team was shocked…but for once, *positively*."

Omar guided Paul to do the following. When he next met Frank, Paul was to say, "Frank, I really want to acknowledge you for the way you ran that country visit to Thailand. Our team there was really charged up. We had, as ever, an incisive review of our competitiveness and plans, but you really left them feeling good about moving forward."

As they had planned, Paul was emphatic and hugely enthusiastic and grateful as he shared this with Frank.

Frank was taken slightly aback as Paul wasn't usually so expressive. He replied, "Good, good, but you seem to stress *Thailand* so much. We did eight visits. What about the rest?"

And this was exactly what Omar had helped Paul to anticipate. Paul was ready with a clear answer that wouldn't affront Frank, "Well, they were fine in the usual sense, but Thailand, *Wow*, that really delivered in a big way—that's what country visits are all about."

Frank now was deeply intrigued. "But the others…"

Paul stayed on script. "Well the others were okay, but you know the Thai team is still buzzing…"

Frank was hooked. "Well, damn it, I'm glad, but what about the others? What was it that made this visit to Thailand so different, so productive?"

And now Paul had been *invited* to provide feedback. But taking a leaf from Marshall Goldsmith's terminology and the paradigm that rightly accompanies it, Omar had prepared him to offer "feedforward" instead. This is a future-focused opportunity rather than a backward-looking critique.

Paul said: "You did so well what I and the team are hoping you'll continue to. You listened, you asked questions, you built on people's ideas, you encouraged people for good work, when you challenged you never did it in an adversarial way, but you retained that wonderful edge you have (which was quite true) which makes everyone re-look at their assumptions."

And that opening comment started an enriching, non-combative dialogue about how to make country visits excel.

Paul reported that in the following year, not only did the region prosper, but team morale and passion also flourished, as

Frank became far more attentive to the "impact" of his visits and not just their "output."

So whenever you catch your boss doing something right, even approximately right, acknowledge it.

Do so by being specific about what you are acknowledging, so it doesn't come off as kiss-ass obsequy. But don't await perfection from your bosses. Rather when they veer in the right direction, tell them! By letting them know **what** you are praising, **why** it made a positive impact and **how** it helped, you will create positive motivation for the bosses to repeat it for two reasons.

First, everyone—even the bosses—like to receive praise. And second, your enthusiasm will invariably get them to compare the situation you are praising them for to other instances when they received either silence, or sullen compliance, or foot-dragging or whatever.

Here's an additional example from a recent exchange that one of us overheard: "Diane (his boss), when you stopped by to thank me for getting that report out in time, knowing as you did that I stayed late to make it happen, I really felt that what I did mattered. I really feel good about that extra effort. Thanks."

Nothing more is needed, but the bedrock of a relationship begins to be laid as those words are said and that appreciation is shared.

Now, how about the other side; about protecting your own passion and taking accountability relative to your relationship with your boss, particularly one whose style doesn't mesh well with yours?

The first change, as with most real changes, begins right in our own head and heart. We have to switch our perceptual apparatus from thinking that our job is to "evaluate" our bosses and "assess" their relative perfection judged by what is most pleasing to us personally. Instead, let's make peace with the realization that we should learn from them whatever we can.

Our job is to make, in Jack Welch's words, our boss smarter because we're on their team. We have to help them win not for political reasons, but because that is the definition of our role. That's what we've signed up for in addition to delivering value for our company and growing our own talent, ability, and prospects.

Assuming your boss is not purely there due to nepotism, patronage, or his own advanced proclivity for "moisturizing" his/her own boss, then they probably have some skill, experience and relevant expertise. You will have many bosses in your career, and you don't have to swoon over all of them. Your job is to learn from them—whatever they can teach.

Now, hopefully being aware of areas where our bosses are not particularly accomplished will keep us from learning dysfunctional things from them. Rather than fretting about their imperfection, we can discover what Noel Tichy has called a "TPOV" (a teachable point of view). And if we can figure out our boss's TPOV and become a student of it, we can leave even a largely dysfunctional boss, having grown in wisdom and insight.

Omar was coaching a chief financial officer (CFO) of a major company who smiled with recognition when Omar made this point to him.

"You're right," said Lars, "my last boss was quite unimpressive in most regards. But he could handle people—he could diplomatically manage the most tense and intense of situations. And while it seemed that's *all* he could do, I have the opposite challenge. I'm a firebrand. And I deeply wish I had spent more time learning how to be effectively diplomatic from him. I may not have used it much, but there are times, dealing with our chairman, various partners, and key customers, that I know it's something I have to develop."

Our job is to learn from each other, not constantly judge each other. And if you are keen to learn from the strengths of your boss, and acknowledge when she does something unusually well (in other words, outside her usual framework), then you can also constructively coax your boss to spread her own wings.

Either way, this combination of approaches allows you to retain accountability in guiding your boss. It also ensures that you get the very best from each one, rather than only gaining from those bosses whose styles and strengths jibe with your own.

In following this approach, we not only liberate mutual passion but also grow ourselves and our relationships.

Taking Accountability for Growing Your Team

As with your boss, the first transformation you need to make when you are trying to get your team to be more accountable is an inner one. Your primary job as a leader is *not* to judge and evaluate people; it is to help them improve. Understanding that, and leading on that basis, is one of the biggest differentiators we know between pedestrian and powerful leadership.

While we stand by that, there is a *proviso*. There is indeed a time of judgment. One of those times is when selecting team members. You should indeed be as selective as you can in terms of talent. You are looking for: the right profile for the job, the right attitude, the fit with company values, and hopefully a measure of constructive iconoclasm. You may even, as Whole Foods does, let potential team members also interview applicants for the job. Whole Foods does this because their workforce is organized into teams that "own" various parts of the store, and are responsible for and are judged, and financially rewarded, on how well those sections perform. Hence, team members have a vested "stake" in each other.

But once the person has been selected, we shift to *leading*. Our job is then to help them fulfill their potential, to deliver and to win.

Two points need to be made here. First, the evaluations have to come *after* a performance period during which the person is not judged harshly for going through a learning curve! In fact, helping them make that learning period as productive as possible is a prime leadership responsibility.

Second, leaders have to be evaluated too. In top global companies, you cannot be promoted beyond a certain level if you cannot show that people who report to you have actually moved into leadership positions of their own. Those leaders who get their people promoted and advanced clearly attract the best talent to their own teams. Their commitment to the success of each team member will be an enormous passion liberator.

At Ricardo Semler's wonderfully precedent-shattering Semco in Brazil, there are no job titles and no offices. They offer true flexi-hours, and radically empower their people. Leaders receive publicly posted performance ratings by their team members. If someone's "leadership satisfaction" ratings continue to sag, the writing is on the wall. They themselves know they have to either radically revise what they are doing, or move on. Fortifying or even perpetuating that status quo isn't acceptable in the Semco culture, nor should it be in any progressive company.

In addition to redefining ourselves as a "talent agent" and "success coach," another remarkably simple and yet passion-*and* performance-fostering initiative that leaders can undertake is being part of something that is called "the mentoring tree."

Here's how it works. Leaders across the company are asked to select someone in the organization that they believe has more capability than they are expressing. Then, without fanfare or official announcements, the leaders privately select that person as someone to be coached, as their own development project. Their challenge, in the next six to nine months, is to help that person deliver at a measurably higher level.

They will undertake to seek them out, engage them, put them into projects and offer them challenges that will develop them; ensure they get the right visibility and acknowledgement for achievement, and become a positive stimulus for them. They are doing that "little bit extra" which is often all it takes to ignite someone of great potential.

This works best if all the senior leaders pick one to two annual mentoring projects. This requires no "program," no HR oversight, no "launch"… you just do it.

Omar advised a major European bank to undertake this. They reported 100 days later that they were astonished by the waves of personal initiative, focused performance improvement, *and* emotional positivity that had come flooding through their organization as a result of this being kicked off by all the senior leaders.

We are astonished why every organization when hearing of this idea, doesn't dash to implement it. There isn't a downside. The upsides include reducing estrangement, getting leaders off their backsides and into the potential-fostering role they're meant to be in.

Creating Your Own Development Team

The ultimate accountability you can claim is for your own growth and development. And by empowering yourself to set up your own coaching network we'll show you how to do that in a minute. You'll heighten relationships as well as focus the natural passion for moving forward that courses through all of us.

Here's what you need to do. Start by creating a stakeholder map. Essentially you list all the people who have a "stake" in, or are impacted by, your work. For example, you would include your boss, direct reports, people in other departments, even any key suppliers or customers if you're willing to reach out to them. This covers anyone who has some say in your success and who can reflect back to you the quality of your actions and interactions.

Make a list of what you think your stakeholders, overall, most want and need from you in terms of leadership, aptitudes, attitudes, and behavior. When we did this recently with a key leader in a financial services company, his initial list included: "Trustworthiness, accuracy, attention to detail, proactive communication, effective trouble-shooting, non-defensively receiving feedback, acknowledgment of contributions, high energy and enthusiasm, industry knowledge, the acumen to solve problems fast."

Based on a number of performance reviews he had received, and guided by Sensei to look at where the most frequent sources of friction were, he prioritized "proactive communication," "non-defensively receiving feedback," and "attention to detail" in that order.

He then went to three key people in his stakeholder pool and bounced these off them to verify he was going to be concentrating on the right behaviors They affirmed his selection, expressing enthusiasm for the effort, even if a little pointedly (hinting that it was high time). But then, it's high time for all of us, isn't it?

Once a few areas for improvement are selected, you simply approach a cross-section of your stakeholders, picking a smattering of fans, a few who are "tepid" towards you, and a few who are "honest critics" (defined as people who are tough on you, but seem to back you when you're right) and say something like, "I just need five minutes of your time. I'm keen to improve my leadership skills. Given the feedback I've received and areas where I can see I'm not making the kind of impact I want, I've selected these top three areas. On any of these, or all of these, do you have a few suggestions for me? I'd really appreciate it."

Three things can happen.

1. They will tell you. In which case, listen actively, paraphrase what you've understood to ensure it's what they meant and say "thank you." Marshall Goldsmith is so right to emphasize that no other response when you *ask* for someone's input is fitting.

2. They will look at you funny, wondering what the catch is. If so, explain why you selected them as a critical stakeholder, and just repeat the question, letting them know that any suggestion that they feel would help would be welcome. Most people will then eke out "something" at least to get the dialogue going.

3. The third thing that can happen is they'll ask for some time to consider it. If they do, peg a specific follow-up, and initiate contact accordingly.

Then each month, when you are having a natural interaction with them (so that you don't have to schedule a "formal review" which will get onerous and irritating for everyone) just say, "You remember I was working on x and y and z and you gave me a couple of suggestions. I really appreciated them. How am I doing?"

No matter what they say, ask for a couple of specifics so you understand what they mean. And then just say, "Now that I've been working on it, do you have any further suggestion or recommendation for me?"

As you do this consistently, a few things will happen. First, it will seem, and will become, natural.

Second, people will realize you mean it, as long as you are consistent in asking for their help and are acting even somewhat on what they have to say, and their trust in you and your overall relationship will strengthen. One of the best ways to help people trust you is to let them teach you something or to help you in some way.

Third, they will tend to notice your efforts, and not only give you better recommendations, but very likely also give you positive credit for your commitment, humility, and follow-through.

Remember since they are stakeholders, they already *have* a view of how you're doing. The only issue is whether you will learn of it in a sober, reflective moment, or only emotionally at moments of meltdown or crisis when neither of you are at your best.

And once it seems the areas you initially selected are advancing nicely, when most people are saying that you are making good progress, then based on the suggestions you are hearing you will naturally develop a secondary list of areas in which you wish to improve. By this time, such conversations will be flowing more and more naturally and you will almost habitually follow-up without having to remember to do so each month.

Another windfall is that some of your stakeholders will likely ask you the reciprocal question as to their own effectiveness.

Earlier we recommended having shared results conversations with anyone with whom you have to produce a result. With the most critical stakeholders, this coaching process can become the follow-up mechanism.

However, you can apply this farther and wider than with those people with whom you're going to have such a detailed exchange and agreement. Anyone who sees you in pivotal moments and has a stake in how you do and how you come across can be invited and inducted as a coaching partner. Take the same approach, and they are likely to be flattered to be invited and are likely to be more constructive in return.

But what about those situations where there is a key stakeholder that you really should make a part of your coaching "partnership" and should perhaps even be having a shared results conversation with, but who has a poor reaction to you?

This is where you can use an earlier tool, the possibility focus.

Omar had to coach a middle-level leader who knew he engendered an almost allergic reaction in a colleague in another department. And because of this, they only communicated with each other under duress, when there was a problem. Not surprisingly, when either of them saw the other coming, they tensed up and adrenalin shot through their systems—they literally saw a problem approaching.

Frequently, one of the reasons for antipathy of this type is that we have the following feeling about each other: "You only carp and criticize, you never recognize what I or my team do well, you're only out to invalidate our efforts."

Therefore we have to defuse and dismantle this perception. That's where the possibility focus comes in. Omar coached this leader to approach his colleague. And he said: "Ali, I realized I've never told you when you and your team get things right, which is often. So thank you for getting the product to us on time, and thanks for making all the last-minute changes, which couldn't have been easy, so well."

Ali was stunned. "So, what do you *really* want?" he said gruffly. After all, he naturally assumed this was a gimmick, some bit of leverage for a really over-the-top request.

As Omar had advised, Tom didn't make any pending requests at that moment but just said: "I wanted to do better as a colleague and share some appreciation. See you." And then he left. He certainly didn't want to create a second-rate Hallmark moment. He had something to say, he said it, and moved on.

Stephen Covey speaks about filling up our own or someone else's self-esteem bank account. Indeed, when we grate on others habitually and vice versa, often we are only making withdrawals from each other's self-esteem bank accounts. And like any account we treat in that way, we then lose credit-worthiness and stay in the red.

By making proactive deposits, we build a relationship. And then once the account is back to reasonable health, the odd withdrawal will no longer be so taxing, or cause such upheaval.

At the next team meeting, Tom, having been on the lookout for what Ali and his team were contributing, pointed out in front of their boss, a recent productivity surge that Ali's people had delivered. Now, everyone was shocked. Tom knew, to pacify his own nerves, that he would only praise that which was genuinely praise-worthy, so he was relaxed. He was not ladling on fake appreciation, he was restoring his balance relative to Ali.

And a week later, after a fairly consistent barrage of relevant and issue-specific acknowledgement, when a problem did come up, Tom went straight up to Ali and said: "Ali, you know I've been working on appreciating the strengths of your team. Well I'm a convert. And here's a problem my own team is facing. In the past you and I have locked horns unconstructively on issues like this, and I'm sure I've jumped to unhelpful conclusions. I really need your help."

By speaking about his own needs, by taking accountability for past communication and impact, and having begun to make genuine deposits in their relationship bank account, Tom elicited a real conversation with Ali.

The first time Ali walked into Tom's office for a cup of coffee and a follow-up chat, shockwaves went through their respective teams. Initially incredulous, seeing the two sharing a coffee, a conversation, and even a few laughs, led to their teams also quickly getting the message: knock off the turf warfare, and get together to get the job done.

Will this always work? No. There may be chronically intransigent people or those who just have decided to lavish their immaturity on you.

But if someone is like that, let's let them prove it. Let's not assume it. And in our experience, most people really don't arrive at work looking to foster their own misery or to inflict it on others as we said earlier. We have to ensure we behave in a way that oxygenates a better paradigm.

Applying This Passion Liberator

Absence of accountability strips us of our latent passion. Using this liberator we take accountability for the future, we stimulate creativity and cooperation by rapid prototyping. We learn how to both coach our boss and learn from them. We shift from being evaluators to success coaches, and we create a powerful community of coaches to aid us in becoming more effective and impactful.

Passion and meaning are both linked to relevant engagement. By claiming accountability for results and relationships we set up the conditions for optimal purposeful engagement. As we do, we help lead ourselves and others powerfully and passionately forward.

CHAPTER 10

PASSION LIBERATOR SEVEN: LIVING VITALITY

In order for us to radiate passion for purposeful performance, we need certain vitality habits. In other words, habits of thinking, acting, interacting, and perhaps even emotionally consorting with the world that amplify passion, energy, and enthusiasm. Moreover, if passion is not to become a casualty of our dedication to produce results (both organizationally and personally), we also need a better handle on our relationship with time.

Let's talk about how we can do both, starting with vitality. Perhaps the easiest way to do that is to give you 20 rules to live by that have emerged from nearly two decades of our global leadership consulting and coaching.

How to Amplify Vitality

Rule No 1: Realize that life is what matters

Business is just an aspect of our larger existence. This perspective will prove invaluable. When we see our life as paramount, as the primary reality, then we will make choices ably, capably and imaginatively. We will empower ourselves to design a life we want to lead rather than just feeling buffeted by numerous external forces. Buffeted we may all occasionally be, but if we've signed up for the experience—at least for now—on behalf of a life we want to lead (again, at least for now), then we can navigate the currents far better.

Rule No 2: Get to know your best times to get various things done

If you're not an evening person, really amplify the value of that by having sacrosanct family and personal time then. Use the mornings to get that exercise in, or clean up some key "to do's" from the day before. The idea is to use your highest energy periods to tackle your most difficult tasks.

And, whenever possible, look for places to either recharge or "get ahead." For example, if you feel a surge of energy on a particular weekend and the family members are otherwise occupied, advance that key project that's been "on hold" for so long, or take some rejuvenating hours for yourself by taking that three-hour bike ride you've been meaning to get to. On the other hand, if on the contrary you're utterly exhausted one afternoon at work, take on some more routine organizational chores instead of frustrating yourself by diving into a challenging financial analysis. Even head home a little earlier that day and fully recharge for the next day.

Leaders manage their energy flows in ways that best deliver their goals and maximize their capabilities.

Rule No 3: Realize that you always have enough time for whatever you REALLY want to do

Beware of saying "no" to people or projects that matter to you, especially when you do so routinely. Saying "I don't have enough time" means it's not a priority, I don't think it's important enough.

The secret to being able to say "yes" to what really matters is to have clarity about what you value most, personally and professionally.

Leadership is about clarity. Our time allocation has to match our real priorities. So if you find yourself repeating "I just don't have the time," ask yourself, "how can I more deeply acknowledge its importance?" Once you do, you'll find the time, and find a way—for what counts to us, truly, we always do.

Rule No 4: Beware of judging life by QUANTITY rather than QUALITY

How "long" you get to do various things often matters less than your engagement, your intensity, your presence, and your commitment to the act. How many hours you work on a project is secondary to the quality of uncompromised attention and focus you bring to bear on it. How many nights at home matters less, than the readiness to interact and communicate and connect that you bring home with you. Even 60 minutes of lackadaisical thrashing in a pool will hardly equal 20 concerted minutes of aerobic laps with a clear target to attain.

If you fritter away concentration, it can take an awfully long time to get only a very few things done. If you optimize your focus, you can appreciate, savor, and contribute to so much.

In personal relationships remember that the heart doesn't tell time, it simply registers impact. Savor a conversation, be fully present to an exchange, and you can create a life-time memory. Simply "occupy space" together day and after day, and you may only accentuate mutual boredom and ennui.

In professional relationships, remember that nobody evaluates hours, they take stock of value received and care extended. Leaders understand it is not the effort. It is the result.

Rule No 5: Get away from being perpetually dissatisfied

Being perpetually upset or dissatisfied is like a personal Geiger counter, it tells you something is indeed "wrong," but INSIDE. If your whole life is one of being perpetually malcontented, you are either someone of extraordinary ability, talent, and standards who towers above everyone else in discernment and perspicacity (congratulations if so!), or else you are transferring inappropriately to the world what you're really upset about, some aspect of yourself! If it's the former (rarer by far, I think, we can all agree), channel the dissatisfaction into growing other people. If it's the latter, spend time to grapple with the only person who can soothe your pain—yourself.

Leaders challenge themselves every bit as much as they challenge others. They know that chronic emotional pain is a "wake-up call" as well as a call to take some different action in key epicenters of our lives.

Rule No 6: Embrace challenges

The much lauded state of "flow," when we are naturally "in the moment," and great performance is heightened, occurs when there's "enough" stress but not too much.

In other words, when there isn't enough challenge, life becomes bland and we get bored.

When the challenge significantly exceeds our current capacity or experience, then we feel fear and tend to get overwhelmed. Both states are counterproductive.

We want enough challenge that we are fully awake, fully alert, and experience a sense of productive urgency. Yet we want enough calm so that we feel we have a reasonable shot at success; or at least a shot at enough partial achievement so that we can then learn through that experience in order to improve dramatically for the future.

So, if you're bored, raise the bar. If you're paralyzed with fear, ask for coaching, additional support, guidance, tools, and help. Let's thereby successively upgrade what we can handle without undue stress.

Leaders remove unnecessary stress so they can thrive on productive challenge.

Rule No 7: Ask "what have I learned" every so often

Always have something you want to read or someone you want to talk to (depending on the situation), and somewhere to capture inspiration when it strikes.

A great report card of your time is to ask: "What have I learned this year that I didn't understand so clearly last year?" If the answer seems profound, moving, insightful, then your reflection, reading, and interaction must be productive.

On the inspiration or new ideas front, look at how many projects or initiatives you have *completed*. However in evaluating this, look for things that were self-initiated which you then catalyzed and fulfilled, bringing others on board as needed. As the number and impact of these go up, so does our leadership influence.

Leaders learn incessantly and catalyze themselves endlessly.

Rule No 8: Introduce the new, appreciate the old

Try every year to include some new experiences that will vivify your existence. Every year plan to experience again some things you already adore, but truly celebrate them.

Let's look at new experiences first. Put on skis for the first time, or ski a new valley. Take a totally different vacation or break. Read something dramatically different. Immerse in a new culture. Learn to taste wine, or tea from different places around the world perhaps. Interact with someone much younger, or older, than yourself. Start an investment plan, whatever.

On the other hand, have that favorite meal again but stop and savor it. Have that family get-together but discover how to make it a true joy for all those participating. Watch that favorite movie, but shut off the phones, pop the popcorn, and stay in your pajamas all day. Take that favorite hike with your favorite person, but stop and "drink in" the splendor all around you.

Leadership is about creating new and increasing value for others and our businesses. A person who doesn't know how to renew and revitalize personally will always come across as "fake" when they preach re-invention to their team and to their market. Equally, a leader who can't appreciate what's already been achieved, the people already there, the business opportunities already at hand to better leverage, will always underperform—since they can only suboptimally optimize what already exists and is in place.

Leaders remake themselves and their circumstances all the time. They also get more value from existing strengths, abilities and relationships than most people considered possible.

Rule No 9: The attitude of gratitude

Look around at your life. It is enhanced by all kinds of people who probably don't know how much they mean to you, or how highly you value them. Take some time to let them know. It doesn't have to be a gift or a "thank you" card, though of course those can be deeply appreciated. It could be some time invested, some support offered, some guidance given, a special experience shared. You don't have to say, "This is because..."

Just do it. They'll draw their own conclusions. If you always link generosity to some "reason" for your action, then you continue to lay the foundations for a very *quid pro quo* and conditional relationship. Do it for the joy of acknowledging if not for celebrating the gift of your relationship. Refuse to explain "why." What will then bloom will be something richer than rationale, and anchored in true mutual affection.

If we think about how to enhance the lives of those we value, *and if we expand our vision so that we can value more people*, we will initiate a virtuous cycle of appreciation, shared understanding, and mutual commitment.

Leaders create teams, allies, and collaborators wherever they go.

Rule No 10: Say what you have to

It's not leadership, but hypocrisy to go underground with your animus, anger, annoyance, irritation. However, first shout it out privately, blow it off, walk around the block, and THEN say what you want to others.

When you do, remember there's a difference between emotion and meaning.

By all means, say what you feel and what you mean, but make sure you leave the room open for some healthy doubt rather than stating it as an adamantine certainty. Don't share your personal opinions as facts.

Great leadership teams are built on trust. When that goes, everything goes. So while leaders are careful to say what they really feel and really think (not necessarily just their first reflex), they ensure they DO say it. They expect and encourage others to do likewise.

Rule No 11: Be here, now

Be here, now (and nowhere else) adds to and augments the fourth vitality habit and applies EVERYWHERE in life.

Don't go to breakfast with the family, and be lost behind a newspaper. Don't attend a child's sporting event, only to be on the cell phone the whole time. Don't kiss your spouse, while planning your morning presentation (or vice versa)!

When coaching someone, truly coach them rather than checking out your haircut in the reflection of the filing cabinet. When preparing a written communication, commit to giving the audience of that communication full value, rather than listening out of the corner of your ear to the latest football score.

When taking a break, TAKE it! If you're at a spa, don't replay your last customer exchange. That way when you get to your next customer exchange, you'll bring all your attention to bear there, not on how stressed and worn out you are.

Rule No 12: Recharge, regenerate

Pick something that matters to YOU, and do it for at least some time each week. It needn't be lofty; it doesn't have to produce social value. This is your regeneration and recharge activity. It could be a hobby, it could be viewing a favorite program, it could be time alone with music, it could be painting, it can involve a walk on the beach, it could be putting your feet up and reading the Sunday comics. But having alighted on this activity or activities, make sure you guard the time as sacred. How long doesn't matter (please see again vitality habit number four on this;), the quality and passion of your concentration DOES.

Leaders look after themselves, so they can look after their organizations and teams.

Rule No 13: Challenge the unproductive

Make a list of, say, six irritations in your life: messes, annoyances, recurring emotional "spills." Go to war on one each month and liberate untold energy and creativity within six months as these are each either out of your life, better handled, or at least working far more productively.

Here's an example of what we mean. A colleague of Omar's reported that he was beside himself because his laundry man stapled identification tags to his clothes. When he grabbed for his clothes in a hurry, this produced aggravation, and the risk of damage. After fuming for almost a year and cursing the fates, he simply told the laundry service: "Find another way to do this, or lose my business." He also showed them his laundry receipts for 12 months, totaling about $1,000. He now gets safety pins from them! He has gained the convenience he sought, and they continue to have his business. This is a seemingly trivial example. But multiply this by a number of unnecessary absurdities in life, and it becomes quite significant because like our houses, the foundations of our peace of mind are sometimes brought down by the termites rather than the tornadoes.

Leaders know how to clean up messes and challenge unproductive trivia.

Rule No 14: Reach out to others by reaching "in" to them

Make a personal connection with key service staff, especially those situated so as to be able to help you. These include bank tellers, airline staff, hotel receptionists, waiters, customer service people, etc. Let them know you "see" them. Personalize your interactions by calling them by name if possible. Engage them as if they were top professionals seeking to help you. As you become "human" to them, they will work harder to find a way to help you. If they can't, they'll at least care enough to look for the next best alternative. No one likes to let down a good opinion someone has formed of them.

Don't wait to form such an opinion, give them an "A" at the outset, and then let them prove you right.

If, despite this, someone is being indifferent or an outright obstructionist, then become more passionate and insistent, never rude or boorish. Keep raising the intensity, state the case as clearly and as logically as you can, and ASK for some satisfaction or additional service attention if your direct request can't be gratified. If someone then digs in with an unproductive indifference, either escalate this to their boss or become enough of a nuisance so that it's easier to deal with you then to ignore you.

However, these expedients induce quite a bit of wear and tear. Don't let this be your default position. You'll actually find that in all but some rare instances, reaching out to people will result in their reaching back toward you.

This is practice for engaging key people in your leadership life as well. Speaking to their better angels and then raising the intensity (not hostility or rudeness) in a constructive manner, is the key.

Leaders make it easy for others to help them; they apply constructive pressure only to stimulate creativity and kindle a commitment in others.

Rule No 15: Create opportunities

When having to refuse someone something, if the person and their idea are essentially valuable, always offer options. Here are two examples:

"I'm sorry we can't meet in person this week, because I'm traveling. Can we set up a video conference this week, speak by phone today, exchange emails in the next 48 hours, or schedule an in-person meeting within this month?"

"I'd like to respond to your team request, but I worry about the precedent it would set, if done just for your team. Would you like to make a case for the value and fairness of this, or shall we give various teams a performance-based incentive for such a situation, or can we find another way of responding to your team's concerns and needs?"

Look for multiple options and ask people to *share* the problem with you in resolving the best way forward.

Leaders create opportunities, rather than settling for roadblocks.

Rule No 16: Enhance your travel time

Use travel time wisely. If you fly a lot (as we do), then treat each plane trip as an opportunity. If you learn to meditate and physically relax, you can use the time to catch up on sleep. If you take along material you otherwise never get to, you can get loads of reading done. If you've been meaning to reply to something or work on a project and time eludes you, guard this occasion to work on that.

Catch up on a movie you've missed (either via the options on board or using your own laptop), reflect on your life's goals, sit back and relax. Do some of the things in the air that steal your time (even if it's just planning) when you are on the ground. That will free up energy when you are really with the people and places you want your prime-time energy and attention for.

Leaders use seemingly "dead" blocks of time for "live" purposes.

Rule No 17: Create traditions, celebrations

Plan some mini-trips each year. These can be special weekends or times or occasions that you really "plan." So you think about them, have a shared results conversation with those who are taking this time with you, and prepare to suck the marrow from the experience. It's great if at least one or two of these can be other than the obligatory birthdays or pre-established seasonal celebrations.

When you CREATE your own celebration, or tradition, you have to invest it with your own meaning. You have to decide what you're celebrating. Give it a theme; don't let it be just a mindless ramble. Omar and his wife Leslie do a six-day walking tour in medieval villages on the outskirts of Provence as an annual pilgrimage. It's their time to reconnect, investigate their lives and leadership purpose, and make sure they're heading where they want to. They've made sure the scenery, setting, history, places they stay, all inspire and excite them.

This is now an annual tradition, as is an annual joint-planning day for the year ahead and gratitude for the year past, prior to skiing each year in January.

As two of the partners in Sensei as well as being life partners, Omar and Leslie travel to different countries virtually every week. Therefore they like having "fixed coordinates" for these occasions. For others who spend more time in one place, the need may be for new climes and locales as they plan these special occasions.

Determine your own special places and times. Ritualize it to an extent; they don't have to be the same precise dates, but aiming for around the same time of year helps to cement the clearing in your calendar. You don't have to go to France. You can investigate your own options. You can go work with a guru in India (as a friend of ours does annually), or volunteer for a week with a charitable organization. You can work on beautifying your garden, or learn how to raft over a weekend of shared goal setting. You can take a picnic together and then share some feelings with loved ones. You get the idea...

And if you hear the inner critic saying, "I don't have the time," remember, you can start with long weekends, and then expand options as your life hopefully expands in options and opportunity.

Leaders create occasions for themselves that are alive with meaning and possibility.

Rule No 18: Invite mutual cooperation

When you need to really get someone's attention while conversing with them, and it is not going well and you are aggravating yourself and finding your energy plummeting, try the following. Use a dramatic pause... this stops the chatter, and draws attention.

Then look them in the eye to let them know that what follows really matters. When you speak again raise your voice just slightly for emphasis. Say what's most relevant first. Share what you feel as your personal feeling, not a cosmic certainty. Invite mutual exploration, and suggest some next steps that you feel will be important together. This would work particularly well with the advice we've offered relative to preparing for and sharing radical conversations.

Ensure you *listen* as well as speak. If the person is addressing something other than what you've raised, empathize and replay what you've understood, then gently request that you'd appreciate a continued focus on what you had raised, at least initially. You can then move on to other topics subsequently.

When they ARE addressing what you've raised, try to listen for "possibility" in what they're saying, but be really clear, honest, pragmatic, and action-oriented. The more abstract you are, the more people's eyes glaze over, or the more cerebral (rather than passionate and committed) they become.

Relative to feedback, don't generalize. It is far better to say, "I'd really appreciate if I can complete what I'm saying," rather than, "You never listen, you just want to butt in and say what you want."

Say, "I worry because we made a commitment, and it didn't happen from your end as far as I know, and you never let me know. How can we make this better?"

This is far better than, "You never keep your commitments, I'm not sure I can trust you, why don't you ever let me know?"

Leaders connect, communicate, invite, and ignite shared action.

Rule No 19: Raise the quality of your being

Spend a little bit of time *preparing* for certain aspects of life, including being ready to be able to experience the richness and variety of what life has to offer. The more we learn, to some extent, the more expansive our paradigms, ideas, emotions, and possibilities become.

So, for example, Joseph Heller's *Catch 22* on the absurdity of war should be read by everyone. If you're in Hanoi, you may find a classical Western opera playing at their splendid opera house. Read a classic book (Milton Cross and Karl Kohrs for example) to understand the major operas, so you don't sit there resolutely wishing Tosca would hurry up and toss herself off the roof to speed up proceedings. Read about new places you visit, you'll appreciate more of what you see. Spend extra time when entertaining, to think about how to truly "treat" the people you're taking out in terms of the right setting, ambience, cuisine, and even tempo of the evening.

Before a key meeting or engagement, think about WHY it's being held, what it needs to achieve, and how you can best contribute in a collaborative rather than "showboating" manner. This will palpably affect the quality of your preparation and then your attention, responsiveness, collegiality, and constructive enthusiasm for moving things forward.

Leaders get ready to suck the marrow from life and build the aptitudes and appreciation that allow them to do so!

Rule No 20: Put yourself on the line, accept the outcome

When you have to perform on behalf of others (provide service, chair a meeting, deliver a speech), arrive EARLY. Get psyched. Prepare emotionally, not just mentally. Think of the two to three key things you want to convey, or get right, or deliver. Do your very best. Energize people by your eagerness to improve and add value. Make it about THEM, not about you. Put yourself on the line and bring ALL of you to the occasion.

Then, go home, forget about it. No one event should determine your self-esteem. After forgetting about it for a while, remember it, and decide how you want to do better next time.

But the fate of global civilization probably does not hinge on this one performance, speech, or meeting. If you think it does, you will freeze up, choke, and your creativity will flee. Keep perspective, and treat it all as a growth and contribution adventure.

We need time and space to be emotionally ready to be at our best. Leaders use each occasion to LEARN and AMPLIFY their value.

So there they are. With these 20 vitality recommendations (with your own adaptations of course), life will work better, work will flow better, you'll appreciate more, give more, perhaps even become more. There can't be a better ambition than that!

These passion liberators are another way to ensure passion killers don't have the last word.

Tackling the Time Tests

The best way to utilize the vitality habits above is to not only review them personally but to review them with your team. Encourage every one to name at least one, and no more than three, of the habits, or arenas in their lives that they need to make progress in.

If each team member consciously moves the goalposts in one to two areas per quarter, the energy and passion liberated will be tremendous.

We recommend that the time tests be taken on next. The reason is that the vitality habits are a foundation and the time tests are focal areas where our stimulated and released energy can be best utilized.

Here are 10 that have proven useful to us.

1. **Create a "to don't" list.** From it, pick two of the things that sap your time and energy and don't add value that you can influence and remove. Go to war on two each quarter. As

they go, our energy and excitement grow. This can be a pointless meeting, a useless monthly report that is mindlessly generated, a ponderous process that saps energy or a recurring set of customer complaints whose root cause needs to be addressed. If you find two stellar candidates for removal, but think you can't influence or remove them, find out who can and create an influencing strategy. Find out what they are trying to achieve with these activities and demonstrate how it could be better achieved, always speaking in terms of their interests as well as yours.

But don't be a smart aleck or share this "truth" at all condescendingly. Help them "arrive" at the idea and help them write their own victory speech at this breakthrough if necessary.

2. **Show up for key interactions determined to bring up conversations you want to have**. If someone says, "This is not the time," politely ask for when would be a better occasion, opportunity, and then follow up. Thereby you build a brand as someone committed to speaking truth (albeit diplomatically when you can) to power and making things happen.

This is not just being contrarian. We're suggesting that you pick the largest, most adaptive, most constructively provocative conversation to ignite in each and every meeting, for five specific reasons.

- You'll have a blast.

- You'll help everyone else. Odds are you are not the only one who believes these issues should be raised.

- If your leaders have any mettle, they'll cherish you for it.

- You may just stop being invited to meetings that aren't meant to advance anything, but which are just pro forma.

- Finally, you'll come alive, and your faculties, attention, and energy will all be heightened.

3. **When someone calls, be pleasant for sure, but let them know the boundaries of your current attention and availability**.

"Hey Suzanne, got a minute?"

"Sure John, my next meeting isn't for another 10 minutes. How can I help you in that time?"

This isn't being rude, or officious. It's just letting people know what time you can dedicate right there and then.

Life is time. Waste one and you waste the other. And by having a sense of urgency about time, you will gain enough of it, such that for the occasions you choose, you can put the wristwatch away and just wallow in your chosen experience.

Funnily enough, by letting people have a boundary, you help train them to be more precise, concise; to have their thinking in order, to make clear requests, and to be ready to engage.

Similarly when calling on others, just ask them what they're in the midst of, and suggest a time boundary yourself. "Gopal, I need 30 minutes of your time to crack this project impasse. Is this a good time? If not, can you let me know when this week?"

This is much better than a general request for a chat over a cup of coffee at some unspecified date which will usually then await being triggered by the advent of a crisis, while nibbling away at the periphery of your consciousness in the interim.

4. **Always have your day packed** with not only the "have to do" items, but some "choose to do" (high value proactive options that are more future-creating as we have spoken of earlier) and "will do if I can" items (worth doing, but less of a priority or impact right now). Really distant prospects or "maintenance" tasks can be procrastinated without much of a guilty conscience, or better yet delegated. Then when the unexpected happens, which it almost always will, you can sacrifice the "will do if I can" items without remorse, while hopefully protecting the other two.

Getting the "have to do" items done is inescapable. But advancing the "choose to do" each and every day, making measurable progress in high value areas which we opt to initiate, is the very essence of leadership.

5. **When you have an important project gathering dust because everything else clamors for attention**, try this. Take 30 minutes and as fast as possible, make as much progress on it as possible. Take as many decisions, write a first draft, and distill salient points. Leave it in a shape such that you can pass it on to your team or colleagues to move further. Maybe they can't finish it without another round from you, but in 30 minutes you can leave it in a state that can be worked on and advanced by others.

   Then when it's next stalemated, book another 30 minutes, and blitz it again. Make sure you assemble all the people/materials/information needed to immerse yourself; take key decisions, provide guidance and move on.

   These "30 minute chunks" are much easier to find than a half day or even several hours and via this you can unblock virtually anything.

6. **If you are an executive with global or even regional responsibilities,** when you next negotiate a raise or a shift in role, decide how many days you can sensibly travel and build that into your package of agreements.

   If they insist they need more travel time than you want, have them first demonstrate that your company is taking full advantage of all existing technology, virtual team-working options and teleconferencing, among others. If the company can show it is doing everything feasible, and there is still a real need, have a discussion. Otherwise, it's an insult to your intelligence and your life.

   One way to reduce your amount of travel is to offer to help lead a project to help the organization achieve its aims of say a 30% reduction in travel, and ask for a senior-level champion to bolster and commit to the effort.

   Since the dividends will be heightened morale, sharper communication (to avoid another remedial meeting), better follow-through AND lower costs and less wear and tear, there is a significant business as well as human case to be made here.

   A company unwilling to negotiate this is saying leaders are disposable piston rods. Help your company come to a different conclusion.

7. **The greater our energy, the faster and better we can get things done.**

    Time "off" used constructively leads to time "on." Whatever your natural "joy producers" are, schedule them as abundantly as you can each week and for longer periods when you can. If longer is not possible, then try consistency. The recurring nature of these recharges stockpiles into almost equivalent personal value. So this might be things like an evening hour with loved ones over a glass of wine that is virtually inviolable, a Sunday morning hike, movie night, a ritual of bagels and freshly roasted coffee with the Sunday paper, reading stories to the kids, whatever.

    Even while traveling, create your "recharges." This may be a workout at the gym, a visit to a local museum, catching a film or music festival, a visit to a distinctive restaurant, some extra sleep, a different exercise class, a spa treatment, or exploring a new town.

    Yes, being on the road you may be lonelier. But delightful time in your own company, rather than sterile surroundings, is still restoring. Activities open us up; they allow us to bring more of us back to those we really care about.

    Moreover, many "recharges" (beyond sleep anyway) tap a range of our faculties. Engagement hones us, while monotony drains us. And as we are stimulated, we'll carry that sharpness and edge into the work we're there to do as well.

8. **Don't engage in pointless debates**. As we've said, consult often, and early. That way people have an investment in your idea and don't feel they have to showcase their value by nitpicking what you've come up with.

    In the vitality habits, we've already advised how to get people's attention in a dialogue. But if stuck in a debate going nowhere, ask the person if it would be possible to summarize what you think they're saying. Once you've done so and they agree you've understood them fully, invite them to reciprocate. You can simply say you want to ensure that both of you has a deep insight into what the other really feels and thinks.

    If they decline the invitation, end the conversation. Because they are then in effect staying they don't really wish to converse.

However, virtually everyone will take you up on this once you've first comprehensively and accurately reflected what they're saying.

After a couple of rounds, the real issue will be clear, and you can have a fruitful exchange in place of the pointless debate.

9. **When reading emails or notes**, convert them into either "points to remember" or "actions to take." If they have neither, toss them.

   When you are doing the writing, the greater the urgency, the more you should lead with the requested actions. Then provide the rationale, and stress any nuances.

   The more proactive your message, the more it is about opportunities rather than today's crises; the more of a brief build-up you should provide to ignite engagement. Then specify the action requested and indicate the follow-up expected.

   For example: "We need to find out why we're losing so much of our top talent. The loss of intellectual capital, the impact on morale, and the costs are staggering. Please create a list of some of our top performers and let's decide how we engage them on this subject. I'd like to create a solution team guided by you, made up of our most cherished team members to crack this. Let's plan to review your list at our weekly meeting. Thanks."

   On the other hand, the more evident the need, the quicker you should get to the point, the action, the issue. "We need to get an answer to our customers about this recurring service breakdown. Please let me have your analysis and suggestion by the close of business today. I know I'm right in counting on you to make sure we recover any lost loyalty."

   Always briefly explain "why" as well as "what." It saves other people from wondering, doing something else as a substitute that won't really work. It also allows them to really help because they then know the real aim.

10. **Rules for communication**: A three-slide maximum for presentations; one page for memos; five minutes for a typical call; and 30 minutes for a non-strategic meeting (unless

additional time for relationship-building is an explicit aim of the meeting).

Sound extreme? Work expands or contracts to fill the time available for its completion. So do our slides, memos, and phone calls. Even if you really need a longer meeting, break it up into 30 minute "result slots" and track its progress and success accordingly.

In fact, I would even advocate creating an "ROI" from each communication, picking metrics that relate to the aim of the meeting and call. That way if no action flows, and there is a disreputable accretion of ROIs from certain meetings, you have a reason to decisively intervene.

The greatest untallied cost in corporate life, argues author and change pioneer Fernando Flores, is the commitments not followed through on. Limit the smokescreens, limit the embellishments, and insist on core messages and tangible accountabilities.

The Common Elements

So what patterns did you detect, in the first two sections of the chapter? Here are the three we'd like to showcase as the best way to apply the underlying wick of this passion liberator:

We have to maximize energy before we can maximize time. Someone bursting with vitality is letting you know they are passionate, on purpose, energized, and enrolled. When you, or someone else, are sagging and lackluster, there is an "energy leak" somewhere. Find out where and let's help each other plug it.

The "leak" can be physical, mental, emotional or spiritual. Physical (energy) leak happens due to a lack of exercise, an illness, inadequate sleep or poor nutrition. Emotional leak happens as a result of toxic relationships, the inability to manage stress, or dubious emotional and social intelligence. Mental leak happens when job demands overwhelm, or as a result of an inability to focus or prioritize, disorganization; or when skills become obsolete. Spiritual leak happens when there is a lack of purpose or meaning; when the stated and lived values become incongruent and when one lacks connection or community.

Here are some ways to regenerate or plug those leaks.

When we experience and learn new things, we continue to re-make and re-imagine the boundaries of our own personality and open up fresh possibilities. We continue to grow into someone new. Our paradigms are more expansive, our openness and curiosity flourish, and we even tend to become a transformational variable in our own environment. Staleness and sameness lead to boredom, enthusiasm-fatigue and worse. Leaders should encourage themselves here and encourage team members to become life enthusiasts, in their inimitable way. A great question to ask each other is: "When was the *last* time you did something for the *first* time?"

We're not suggesting that this becomes a new religion of some type where everyone has to give witness to his or her new adventures. We just mean that we become to some extent what we experience. Look for people who bring a multitude of distinctive and innovative experiences, and ideas and stimuli into work. Then acknowledge, recognize, and celebrate those who do. What people do privately isn't the issue, what resources they bring to us as leaders and contributors, *is*.

Relentlessly identify and focus on the critical few things that will deliver the most value—at home, at work, everywhere. Eliminate messes, distractions, fuzzy communication, pointless meetings and exchanges. Focus your best on the most critical.

These three most fundamental attitudes and aptitudes, along with the specific ideas presented above, can give us the capacity to generate and regenerate the energy and vitality needed to focus and even kindle our passion for leadership and life. As we do this together, we create a vital culture of passionate achievement.

CHAPTER 11

PASSION LIBERATOR EIGHT: APPRECIATING POTENTIAL

The eighth passion liberator is about creating the contexts for the expression of potential. It relates to the encouraging, tapping, maximizing, and focusing of collective and individual talent. Done properly we liberate passion and potential within individuals in our organizations, and in the organizations as well.

Appreciative Engagement

What traps potential in a collective sense? What keeps us from tapping our greatest capacities to add productive value?

If you talk to most leaders today, they will usually tell you that they can identify with each of the following four desires and aspirations:

1. I want to be known through my relationships with others and with the organization; not just as a "role" such as logistics manager or operations director. We all want to have personal value, not be a cog in a machine.

2. I want to be heard, to matter, to feel like I count, that my thoughts and feelings are of meaningful importance to those I work with.

3. I want to share my dreams, and to dream together, and to co-create something of value from those shared dreams while at work.

4. I want to not only do what I'm told, but have the latitude to choose how and where I contribute. I want to volunteer my passion.

While virtually all leaders are enthusiastic in affirming the above aspirations, most would also concede that most work-places and even most teams are far away from being "labs" for, or incubators for any of, the above. Rather as we have said, many workplace interactions stifle or retard these hopes.

The four aspirations above are emblematic of numerous health-fostering leadership approaches that emphasize the co-equal role of constructive inquiry and hearty appreciation.

Like virtually everything of value, these approaches have antecedents. They are legitimized by the tradition they both build on, consciously or unconsciously, and continue.

One of the best mechanisms to transform interactions in the workplace so that they more often provide welcome nutrition for the aspirations above, is what has been called community at work.

We have already spoken of the power of "radical conversa-tions." But those are key, linchpin, root, core conversations about things that can have potentially dramatic breakthrough impact.

What about conversations-at-large? Are we doomed, except in these brave, radical interactions to have apathetic and dehumaniz-ing encounters throughout various organizational "touch points"?

We think emphatically not. That's why the first passion liber-ator was about intimacy and how to foster it. However, even with increasing insight into each other, even with progress on removing our masks and dismantling elements of our defen-siveness, it helps to learn how to make everyday conversations as value-furthering as possible.

How can we build on the intimacy we've hopefully started to establish to create communities of real value at work?

Arguably that need got its first real experiential as well as con-ceptual sponsorship from M. Scott Peck's (the ground-breaking author of *The Road Less Traveled* and *The Different Drum* among others) work on community building. Omar worked extensively and intensively with Dr. Peck and his Foundation for Community Encouragement in the years immediately preced-ing Dr. Peck's death.

The purpose of community building in this sense is to teach teams and groups how to communicate in a way that allows for greater exhilaration, joy, courage; and the fostering of our individual value as well as our collective potential.

By "community," Dr. Peck meant a group of people who had not obliterated their differences but had genuinely transcended them. People who had come together to first "know" each other, and then anchored in that authenticity and shared knowledge, could work creatively, passionately, and powerfully together.

The first stage in that process is what Dr. Peck called "pseudo-community." This is where we all pretend that we already accept and appreciate each other. It is a period of cloying, candy-colored fakeness. It is an artificial sweetness. "Bullshit" would not be too harsh a description. "Your call is important to us" repeated to the point of exasperation, followed by a semi-conscious salesperson who can help you with nothing but who "joyfully" punctuates your frustration with "have a nice day" is the epitome of this.

At this stage, we repeat platitudes rather than communicate; we manipulate rather than connect; or as above, we recite options from a pre-set script rather than really trying to help.

The second stage Dr. Peck called "chaos." The only way to escape from the sugary death above is to get real. And that will be initially jarring and uncomfortable. In short, it will be chaotic. During this stage, we have to realize that conflict is okay, and our leadership challenge is to make it constructive, and to ensure that it's on behalf of things that matter. In ancient Sparta, truth was determined (or so it is said) by who could shout the loudest. And there is a lot of ancient Sparta in today's modern politics and media. But chaos is where something "real" is expressed, in terms of depth, not necessarily in volume. So right wing and left wing zealots in the U.S. who routinely fulminate at each other, refusing to let anyone finish an uncontested sentence without spewing a retaliatory accusation is not what we mean by chaos. This is staged mayhem, not much different than WWE wrestling (the new entity that WWF morphed into). We are talking about the expression, whether loudly or softly, of genuine, heart-felt disagreements. Yes, they often are expressed with upset, but bulging veins and vitriol are not prerequisites at all.

And after the divergent views or perceptions are expressed, for chaos to be productive, we have to be willing to hang in there with each other, past the pain and upset, to some "opening"—to a measure of shared growth. This is leadership's ultimate challenge and perhaps most profound demonstration: determining where our passionate disagreements could most constructively lead us.

The third stage is called "emptiness." Dr. Peck did not mean vacancy or void. Rather emptiness here refers to the creation of new space between people.

Omar and his wife Leslie saw the Pulitzer Prize-winning play *Doubt* some time back at home in New York. It is about the clash of wills and world views between a conflicted and loving priest and a fixated yet fiercely resolute Sister. The author leaves the audience to make up their own mind about who was right. Did the priest abuse the boy? Did the sister initiate an unsubstantiated witch-hunt? Do children need the clarity of an intellectual and moral compass from their teachers primarily, or do they need kindness and understanding? In the context of the play and arguably our lives, legitimate questions all.

The point for us is by being willing to doubt, to not know, to say "yes" to the mystery of leadership and life, we practice emptiness in this sense. We let go of our "masks," of our need to be right and to have others agree with us and be just like us. This is fertile ground for purposeful passion and connection.

And finally, we come to community itself. It's a fascinating achievement. Community is where we as a group of people are simultaneously aware of both task and process. We are not only committed to our targets, aims and goals, but are acutely aware of the paths we are following in trying to make them real. Are we doing it together? Are we communicating? Are we building up people's talents and capabilities en route to making this happen? Is the way we are interacting creating a culture that will institutionalize who we want to be? Is how we are embarking on this task making the next task, the next achievement, easier or harder?

Dr. Peck's work here found extension in the work of Peter Senge of MIT. Senge became famous for popularizing the term "learning organization." He has written voluminously on many aspects of leadership. But for our purposes here, three glitter most.

One is again the fascination with "space." Community building is, in a sense, the creating of space for ideas and interactions; and possibilities and dreams and challenges. Peter Senge and his colleagues talk about first understanding where we are. (We spoke about this in "protecting possibility.") And this also means genuinely listening; creating an *opening* for different visions of reality; for a variety of stories to emerge and be told.

Second, Peter Senge and his colleagues consider communication at its best to be about "meaning-making." The deeper the communication, the richer the meaning we invent and liberate. But it also works the other way. The richer the meaning we invent and liberate, the deeper the communication will be.

To realize collective potential, we must potentially light a fire in each other to invent scenarios we want to live into. Senge and his colleagues have been at the forefront of teaching us to map multiple scenarios of the future as a way to collaboratively look at the implications of today's actions on tomorrow's possible outcomes.

Leaders in South Africa did this very constructively and courageously as they re-invented their reality. When factionalism was at its worse, and the hope of creating a post-apartheid society seemed bleak, leaders from all the various groups jockeying for position came together and mapped out possible scenarios of South Africa's future. They realized the agendas they arrived with led to dead-ends.

They realized after explicitly considering all conceivable scenarios that only one path, a path of reciprocal trust and cooperation, offered any viable hope. Sheer pragmatism made the case. Once persuaded of that, these leaders expressed this conviction back to their followers. Imperfectly for sure, but still impressively, South Africans transcended many of the past hatreds and conflicts that had kept them from moving forward. Tragically, the failure to engage in this manner continues to plague countries all around the world.

Third and perhaps most critically, the approach that Senge and company extol is about "sensing" the future, the possibility; the potential that is trying to emerge from every interaction. In this way, every dialogue can potentially "provoke the future." Imagine if our future-creating context for every conversation was: "Each dialogue will move us forward."

This sounds almost mystical until you experience it. When you do, you realize the concept is to try to sense and to liberate the future that will best manifest a synthesis of our perspectives and hopes in each and every conversation or encounter.

Let us provide an example personal to Sensei. "When we were fishing for a name for the company, we flirted with a number of them," Omar explains. "But as we started listening to each other and sharing our values and convictions, we started hearing things like: 'Blend of east and west; facilitating rather than telling; co-creating with clients,' not being 'experts' but 'guides' for their journey; a teacher who nurtures you... And from my martial arts training and time in Japan, the word *Sensei* (literally a guide for your own journey in any field) emerged. And the moment my partners heard it, they said: "That's it!" They liked its enigmatic sound, its pristine simplicity, what it evoked and connoted. We didn't create the name, we almost rediscovered it in our context."

When we tune in to possibilities that are almost struggling to emerge from conversations about trenchant recurring problems or simply from considering and pooling our aptitudes, we get a sense of the power of this paradigm. Whether it's Muhammad Yunus and the Grameen Bank whose loans to those at the extremities of poverty give them a chance to create lives and businesses (they are now poised to bring Yunus' path-breaking approach to micro enterprise from Bangladesh to the West!) or the design and operational synthesis represented by the iPhone with all the concomitant furor generated by an almost inevitable "next step," we see the power of tuning in to what is almost *trying to emerge*.

When we listen broadly as well as deeply enough, we pick up patterns and clues, lattice-works of possibility. And if we can unify them, see how they connect and inter-relate, then we are building on this aptitude. It would be fascinating if leaders and teams were given this as part of their communication brief or mandate, in addition to just sharing facts or data, or relaying information.

If we think about it, we can see that the earlier passion liberators provide the cultural wherewithal for such breakthrough insights to more routinely crystallize and emerge in an organizational culture.

That doesn't mean we're going to hold a referendum on our overall vision or strategic direction. But it does mean we're going to listen for how to bring them to life each day by being attentive to the tides, currents, and energies present in our workplace interactions. In Socratic terms, we're then able to "midwife" and deliver potentially valuable ideas in service of what we ultimately what to achieve.

Optimizing Individual Potential

This brings us to the key tradition that has fertilized the tapping of potential on more of an individual basis: positive psychology and talent development.

Positive psychology is based on the realization that psychology has too long dwelt in the swamps of the dysfunctional, i.e. what *doesn't work*. Positive psychology looks into how to create peak experiences, achievement and purpose. It does this by studying strengths, not just weaknesses, and success, more so than failure.

Research into talent development demonstrates that we all tend to have a "talent profile," a "unique ability" as Strategic Coach Dan Sullivan calls it. We can usually stimulate our strengths to move towards true excellence. Rarely can we do more with our weaknesses than just to shore them up or move them from "appalling" to average.

Hence, it is far more fruitful in a world requiring prioritization and focus, to concentrate on strengths first and foremost. To take what IS present in a person and help that fulfill its potential. Then, working with weaknesses as a part of that effort is far less wearying and dispiriting.

Many times when we coach people we are asked to help them improve in an area. We are often asked: "Given the above, can there really be any growth?" Oh, yes. But let's be clear. Where coaching is appropriate is where a person HAS potential, but isn't realizing it. So, that someone has the capacity and the desire to be a better communicator; or to make decisions more decisively; or to analyze well under pressure but there are barriers or lack of current acumen holding them back. There indeed, growth and development can be profound.

It has become a badge of faith to say that "talent will find its own way." That is poppycock. Talent needs coaching and mentoring. Even Shakespeare had to learn the language before he could revolutionize it.

This is the paradox. We must appreciate the talent someone has, as a way of energizing what it can become. In the bittersweet movie *Junebug*, a character says with poignant insight: "God loves you just the way you are. But too much to let you stay the way you are." Whatever their theological beliefs may be, leaders have to do likewise.

The Talent Wars, Talent Claim

So does passionate excellence owe more to talent or to committed practice? Since the answer to that question is so critical to leadership, to performance, to teams, to organizational results, let's take a hard look at it.

Some years back, the word "talent" firmly entered the leadership and management lexicon. Marcus Buckingham became the public face of Gallup Research in a strikingly incisive business book called, *First Break All the Rules*. It was clearly a book whose time had come as it roughly coincided with, among other things, the landmark McKinsey study called *The War for Talent*. We had clearly entered a new age in people and performance management. The overdue realization that these studies trumpeted was that people aren't "resources" to be consumed, but at the very least "capital" to be invested, or ideally "talent" to be enrolled and catalyzed.

Buckingham and his colleagues challenged conventional thinking in a variety of ways. To understand the provocative wisdom of their insights, we have to first however be clear on what we mean by talent.

For our purposes here, talent is your natural ability. More precisely, it is a naturally recurring pattern of actions and behaviors that can be productively applied. If it isn't "natural" to you, it isn't a talent. It may be an acquired skill, but not a talent. If it doesn't recur, isn't consistent, and often present, then it is an accident and not an ability. If it isn't revealed regularly in actions and behaviors, then it is wishful thinking. And only productive application makes a capacity worthy of being crowned with the appellation of "talent."

So having a gift of the gab isn't by itself a talent, particularly if it flickers and flames depending on the amount of alcohol or other social inducement you've had. But if you as a sales associate, naturally put people at ease, break the ice when people contact your company inquiring about what you offer, and almost irrepressibly communicate your company's value proposition to anyone and everyone—and if it enthuses you to communicate in this way and these proclivities flow more often than not—then we're probably in the presence of a talent.

With this definition in hand, the talent enthusiasts turned conventional thinking on its head by suggesting for example that we:

1. Hire for talent, not experience.

2. Spend our time on our best people, not our most difficult ones.

3. Provide outcomes, not precise steps, when it comes to telling these talented people how to implement objectives.

4. Not to use just promotions as a way to reward excellence, but expand roles and offer development tracks in line with people's talent.

Very briefly, the key justifications for the claims are as follows.

- **Research and experience** show that those who have talent outperform people of equivalent or even greater experience, not by a small factor, but by as much as 10 to 20 times. The talented hotel manager for example can produce ten times the revenue and customer satisfaction of an average one. Talented customer service representatives will have a retention rate that is 100–200% or more than those of "average reps." Our mistake is that we set performance benchmarks based on the "average," rather than what our most talented contributors show us is possible. Imagine what would happen if we set the base-line according to the truly talented, and recruited, incentivized, and recognized accordingly?

The conclusion is that while experience isn't irrelevant, and certainly more important in certain industries and jobs such as being a pilot or lawyer, the most critical thing to test for, and recruit for, is talent. In other words, look for those naturally recurring habits of mind and heart that produce excellence in a given job or role. This demands then that we develop and continue to hone a "talent profile" for success in key roles.

We can quite readily provide someone with technical training, mentoring, and experience. But virtually nothing will breathe into them inspiration, imagination, and natural drive for a particular type of work, or industry, or accountability.

- **Usually we pay attention to what is broken**. And so we spend the bulk of our coaching and development energy on those who aren't performing. We hope to bring them "up to the average." And if we do, we consider that a huge success!

  At the same time we estrange, alienate, or often ignore the really talented. They often also need guidance and encouragement, would respond fantastically to coaching and mentoring and to receiving the prime-time energy of the top leaders. The ROI we get with them would be off the charts! Helping the best get better should be what leadership is about.

  Those who don't display capacity, as opposed to a temporary slump in performance, need to get less of our attention.

- **When we deal with people who don't have a talent for a particular role**, then we have to provide extremely detailed, precise steps that allow for no deviance or novelty. This is a mass production model and isn't very attractive once we cultivate talent and very likely inadequate for the 21st century where fast-response, flexibility, and often seat-of-the pants innovation in response to escalating expectations is demanded.

  Of course neophytes, no matter how gifted, do need models of excellence. Pavarotti had to learn the musical scale, and Tiger Woods had to understand the mechanics of a golf swing, and Bill Gates had to be introduced to a balance sheet. However, beyond learning such fundamentals, people of talent begin to improvise away from the "official" way to their own approach—they adapt, they experiment, they customize. And if we straightjacket them too much, we won't get the soaring breakthroughs we should.

So we need to be very precise and clear about expected outcomes and quite unambiguous about priorities and measures of success. We need to also ensure that people are aware of what has worked before, and what the basic models in the field are. But then while holding them absolutely accountable for the outcomes, we have to allow talented people to develop their own style or approach and not hem them in with the one "official" way we have seen work. Otherwise the limits of our own vision or experience becomes the limit of the possible. Talent has to be allowed to pave new pathways to success for us.

No two great sales people sell in precisely the same way; no two great communicators write or speak with the same vocabulary or structure; no two musicians wield their instruments or interpret a piece in exactly the same way. *Vive la* difference!

- **The old model was if someone excelled you promoted them**. As long as they went higher up the hierarchy, we rarely investigated if their talents and abilities fit the new role. For example, someone may be technically gifted, but managerially hopeless. So now, in the old way of doing things, we thank them by "promoting" them to a management role when they are abysmal people managers. And while they are frustrated, and frustrate countless others, the company loses the cutting edge of their technical talent, expertise, and experience.

  It should be possible to gain rewards, respect, and success in any role delivered with excellence. There can be, for example, a technical track as well as a leadership track. And it should be possible to gain in prestige and financial rewards, and even in challenging roles within your area of specialization. And even for those who have the capacity to be leaders, we should look at their precise leadership abilities ("leadership" being a vast continuum) and promote or move them to jobs that most mesh with those talents.

So if someone is detail-oriented but not turned on by ambiguity, then sending them to explore and open a virgin market for which there isn't a known approach, may not be the best "promotion." However, if a visionary leader HAS opened a market already, and now more discipline and systems and processes are needed by her successor, then this may be an EXCELLENT promotion. Particularly if we help our newly promoted leader create a team around her of naturally enterprising people who can supply some of the innovative idea generation talent and chutzpah this person may lack.

We have to design roles and even configure and grow teams so that there is a medley of complementary talents and everyone has a chance to do what she does best most of the time, in situations that will allow her to develop that capacity to world-class levels. Then, we all thrive and passion will be abundant, natural, and productive! Seen in this vein, it is clear why one of the primary jobs of a leader is to recognize, develop, coach, manage, and channel talent, individually and in effective teams.

The Other Side of the Puzzle

The argument that talent is all that matters seems compelling. But is it? The argument seems to imply that experience is irrelevant, that people just don't really develop (all they do, it is claimed, is sharpen their talents), that processes and discipline are always inevitably stifling, and that if success isn't forthcoming it must be the role and its "fit" that are to blame, not the person.

Moreover, people seem to take "talent" as a suggestion that if you have it, you are destined for success. You can hold on to the coat-tails of your talent and let it carry you forward.

But British researchers have pointed out that the Warren Buffets and Tiger Woods, the Bill Gates and the Yo-Yo Mas, doubtless had and have great gifts. But these gifts became "talents" (i.e. were applicable at extraordinary levels consistently) only after years of often tedious, unromantic, unrelenting application and practice.

The researchers refer to "the 10-year rule." Even child prodigies, average nine to 10 years of intensive application and study before they show more than remarkable "promise" and actually generate results in line with their talent. There may be the odd "Mozart-esque" exception, but we can't draw conclusions about human performance based on such a rarity.

Of course the researchers realize that hard work by itself can't be the key. There are people who have devoted much time to areas where they remain confirmed mediocrities.

But what the researchers found is that those who improved engage in what they described as "deliberate practice." Activities are set up in ways to precisely engender improvement. Each time practice is engaged in, standards are set, new ways sought, results measured and tracked, and better ways forward minted.

So if you just kick soccer balls at a goal that won't qualify. If you aim to practice putting 80% of your soccer shots in say the upper right-hand corner of the goal from various angles, observing results, and making key adjustments, that will create a base of applicable skill. Giving presentation after presentation to your team won't make you a compelling communicator. But aiming, for example, to create some ACTION from each speech, even one key, relevant, business-furthering action from the team, and judging each presentation on the basis of how much it gets people to take stock and then take action, would be a way to become the type of communicator who gets people to march forward toward a goal.

So great performers DO work harder. The top violinists average 10,000 lifetime hours of practice compared to 7,500 for the next-level, 5,000 for the next-level after that, and so on. The same applies to the greatest surgeons. These people tend to always challenge themselves to *improve various indicators* of great performance in their field *through practicing.*

Moreover, if we are after results—except in a few fields where a certain raw talent, for example kinesthetic intelligence (physical acuity) for surgeons, or a predisposition to respond to rhythm (for musicians), is probably indispensable—is it the case that those with the most innate ability always perform the best?

Hardly.

We all know of talented underperformers whose talent has been glimpsed but not fulfilled. We know teams made up of great players who haven't practiced AS a team, or synergized their abilities and as a result end up flopping against more average players who have truly collaborated and parlayed each other's abilities powerfully and decisively. The U.S. basketball team in recent Olympics debacles alas, or the British soccer team in the last World Cup, come to mind as instances.

Here's another example. Michael Jordan, recognized by many as the greatest basketball player who ever lived, was cut from his high school team. If natural ability was primarily behind the skill he developed, surely that would have been unlikely. It is interesting to note that even after Jordan became a star, he practiced relentlessly; fellow players commented that he gave each practice shot virtually the same intensity as if he was taking it with the game on the line.

Deliberate practice shows up yet again! The business application of this insight is that when you face your daily tasks, don't just try to get them done, try to do them *better* each time in discernible ways that will add real value to what you are doing overall.

So, decompose a task. Writing a presentation involves research, analysis, engaging others to get additional insights, creating a way of conveying conclusions, and delivery. Each of these skills is improvable.

Jack Welch arguably became the unofficial emeritus professor of business leadership because he did precisely this. He took budgeting, for example, and improved how he and his team did it. It became a "swing for the fences" exercise and a way to allocate resources for breakthroughs, rather than a "negotiation" that landed the iterative "last year plus 10%" that is the bane of so many businesses. He took people management, and included 360-degree assessments, talent reviews, coaching, ranking of people each year, among others. He created processes that allowed for "deliberate practice" in the art of leadership. All turnaround masters, Louis V. Gerstner in the U.S. or Allan Leighton in the U.K., excel at this.

Andy Grove of Intel and Bill Gates of Microsoft both have indicated how to make this replicable and portable. Hungry for feedback, and creating multiple feedback loops and reality-checks throughout the business, top business leaders like these use the feedback they get from their practice, to create mental models of what works in their industry and what doesn't. As it becomes clear what delivers results, then we have to consistently, fervently, and with passionate focus, DO, and practice, those things with all the energy and imagination we can.

So is it Talent or Practice?

Noel Tichy who worked with Jack Welch at GE, has been a professor and performance coach for over 30 years in various guises, and is recognized worldwide as a leadership expert. Tichy says that after 30 years of working with managers, even he doesn't know why some individuals engage in deliberate practice and others don't. In other words, he doesn't understand why some people are so much more motivated than others.

And there's the rub. The earlier definition of talent wasn't complete, that's where the confusion has arisen. *Talent IS the very need to practice* in a field where our abilities are such that the ROI on such application is significant. There are increasing returns to scale, perhaps not immediately, but in time.

Even if externally the results take their time to show up, internally we feel ourselves making strides each time we engage, and so within us, it gets easier to show up fully as each forward stride, however miniscule, is experienced.

Talent isn't just the *possession* of naturally recurring abilities that are productively expressed in actions and behaviors. It is the *desire*, the *will* to *develop* and *express* such abilities more productively and capably.

We can all agree that the need is for leaders to help us light our own flame. But they also need to channel our energy in arenas where we are predisposed to be interested, where we learn relatively quickly, and therefore will achieve the "quick wins" necessary to not just coast, but to make ongoing application and commitment into consistent winning habits.

The four points made by Buckingham and company are essentially correct—with the caveats we've provided above. What is often not glimpsed is that talent provides the natural motivational drive *because we experience joy from the **engagement** not only from achievement.*

Grueling as the engagement may be, in such talent-rich arenas, we sense we CAN do it, and that drives us forward. On the other hand, in arenas where our hard work will at best make us "average," we have to wrestle ourselves to make even modest gains. Yes, it may be character building to do so and even necessary to some extent. But if the bulk of our time is spent in such pursuits, then our energy flickers, our larger abilities are deadened, and our vital spark is misapplied.

Because a Tiger Woods can almost "sense" the golf shot he knows he can make one day, because a Pavarotti can almost "hear" the music that can one day emanate from him, because a Gerstner can almost "see" the company he can help IBM once more be, because a surgeon can almost "feel" how to make a currently impossible procedure possible, that inner longing and sense of knowing drives the relentless application and exploration of these world-class performers. That sense, when enlivened by the belief in what they can do, and yet grounded in the humility to acknowledge all they have to learn in order to even be eligible to have a shot at that vision, is the animating spark of real talent, perhaps even its true essence.

The Leadership Opportunity

What does all this mean to you?

As a leader you have to go for talent as having primacy over just an accretion of years. Look more at what someone has *gained* from the experience, not just the fact of the experience. That will be a great clue as to the person's talent here.

Definitely, spend more time developing the best. Always allow for new ways to deliver original championship performances within defined boundaries of ethics and customer needs and profitability.

Absolutely, design roles to fit people, so we allow people to deliver for us while winning personally. As we design roles that will challenge the best abilities that people have, we can then demand that they devote themselves to true excellence, not just acceptable, even if "natural," competence.

But remember the need for deliberate practice, even for the most talented. In fact if people aren't excited by this and don't in some ways almost relentlessly initiate this, they really can't BE talented. Talent is as much the drive to express potential as the mere possession of it. People without this dimension won't hang in there all the way to mastery.

To foster as much growth for as many talents as possible, help people get absolutely clear feedback. A musical note or a basketball shot gives instant feedback. You either hit the note/shot or you don't. Perhaps that's why great performances are more readily summoned in those contexts. In its own way, business needs to create transparent, vivid feedback loops, ones which are ***designed to foster improvement and further deliberate practice.***

Distill models of what works and what doesn't, not from the average, but from the collective, cumulative, living experience of talented people working both individually and in teams. Share those models, not as absolutes, but as guidelines and benchmarks. Yes we want innovation, but we also want people to innovate from understanding not ignorance.

As a key point, those who have a "talent" for working on teams, evidenced by their desire to practice the very improvable skills that will make for team success, should also be recognized. When talent can collaborate, it multiplies and true magic occurs.

Finally, don't reward people by putting them in roles that underutilize them. As we've said, design roles that will challenge the best abilities that people have. And then demand that they devote themselves to real mastery, not just acceptable, even if "natural," competence.

Robert Frost wrote once about the twin compulsions for work: love and need. His conclusion has to be ours as leaders liberating passion through recognizing and stimulating talent. He wrote:

> Only where love and need are one,
> And the work is play for mortal stakes,
> Is the deed ever really done,
> For Heaven and the future's sakes.

Talent is where love and need become one. We love to do what needs doing, and are willing to do what we need to in order to become the caliber of contributor we envision.

Leadership is about creating contexts and roles and challenges and encouragement that make more likely for all those who are willing to rise to this core challenge: namely, to learn to express their best as they continue to develop it.

Applying This Liberator

By appreciating each other, but also being truthful with each other, we find the will and drive to create communities of talent. By listening deeply, by generating scenarios and being attentive to a future that we are literally making feasible through our interactions, we actively welcome and perhaps even usher in our larger collective potential.

But potential also has a critical, inescapable individual component. Here we have to help people build on their strengths first, and encourage them to fortify weaknesses as a way not to blunt the cutting edge of their talent. We have to lead and coach in a way that honors both talent and what it can make possible, as well as the energy to improve and to practice which rescues talent from potentially futile vainglory.

Passion flows abundantly when as leaders and team members we ensure that potential is stoked, supported, furthered, and fulfilled rather than inhibited, intimidated, frustrated, or embattled. The need to get the best from our teams as a whole and from the greatest capabilities of each individual is what makes this passion liberator so vital.

CHAPTER 12

PASSION LIBERATOR NINE: COACHING FOR PASSIONATE GROWTH

The final passion liberator, and the one that brings us full circle, has to do with coaching each other's success.

We liberate passion and liberate our optimum performance when we become our own coaches, as well as further each other's peak performance.

The Great Do-Be Debate

One of the most pronounced dividing lines in leadership and management practice is what we have termed the "do-be" debate. It is a conundrum that if worked through can give us tremendous insight and impetus in all leadership development efforts.

As with the talent debate outlined in the last chapter, the best way to understand the points of view on either side is to find some exemplary voices. We've picked two of the world's top thought leaders.

The first is Marshall Goldsmith, one of the world's most famous executive coaches. His approach to behavioral change revolves around highly focused and specifically measurable growth relative to one or two key behaviors that are dulling the cutting edge of someone's excellence and very likely dampening the passion of those they interact with and have to influence.

The second is the Arbinger Institute. In a series of best-selling books, they have offered a profound alternative paradigm that has had everyone from Stephen Covey to leading CEOs cheering from the rafters. Their essential view is that the problem is not what we do, but who we are *being* as we do it. For them, the intention we have towards other people, based fundamentally on the way we **see** both ourselves and others, is the fulcrum for leadership and interactive effectiveness.

So let's take a deeper look at these two highly substantive and credible viewpoints and see where the dividing line actually is. Moreover, let's explore how they can perhaps even jointly guide us to strengthen our own attempts to tap passion and uncork our best leadership aptitudes.

We are Our Behaviors

This approach is frankly very compelling. How do we know anyone's character (often defined as action consistently taken over time), much less real intention (as opposed to pipe dreams or wishful thinking), except by how they behave?

In our global consulting practice, we ask leaders who interact together regularly to do what Marshall would call a "feed forward" exercise, for us a version of the shared results conversation. Essentially, we ask them to make a request of each other, to offer suggestions for improvement in the future rather than railing and wailing about the past.

We have them imagine it is six months hence, and the other person has positively surprised or "wowed" them. We ask them to consider what would allow that to be true. We then support them in following up with each other and seeking to support each other's success. Unlike a classic shared results conversation which is self-initiated and usually covers our primary relationships, this is done for more issue-specific situations.

In a Sensei session some months back, two leaders faced each other as part of this exercise. They had up to now, alienated and estranged each other. One of them said: "You would *Wow* me if you would hear the complete idea before you conclude whether you agree with it or not."

Having taken some time to digest this and take this on board, when the other one's turn came, he said: "You would *Wow* me if I hear more than just critique, if you could also let me hear what I do right." In other words, they were telling each other what would constitute **evidence of real growth**

and commitment. Behavior is finally how we prove ourselves to each other.

Another supportive perspective here is that as we go up the seniority ladder, the problems we have, the barriers to greater effectiveness, are almost always behavioral. At such altitudes, technical deficiencies have almost always been already weeded out. People who have scaled such organizational heights aren't hindered by lack of technical capability or aptitude.

Hence it is their *expression of their expertise*, the way they collaborate (or not); the way they mobilize and develop their teams (or not), and the way they foster an optimal results culture (or not) that make or break their progress from that point on.

If that is so, why attempt the uphill and daunting task of remaking an entire personality? To do so requires extraordinary will from the person themselves, a concerted dosage of counseling and coaching, and perhaps a raft of other interventions that may be so invasive and time-consuming that the person's life would grind to a halt. That isn't to argue that such journeys of redemption or evolution aren't ever worth it when we feel called to make them. Far from it. But they can hardly be the mainstay of mainstream leadership development—we are running companies not monasteries.

But for practical, results-oriented leadership effectiveness, if we can find the limiting, inhibiting, counter-productive behaviors and shift them, we can get the most efficient and perhaps most effective ROI in terms of liberating both passion and leadership effectiveness along with it. And as success breeds success, the ripple effect of this growth can be remarkably far-reaching.

But how do we produce this shift? Essentially it is similar to the stakeholder approach we sketched earlier. The primary levers are:

- getting feedback from credible viewers and constituents, specifically people affected by this person's leadership and team behavior;

- prioritizing from the feedback, the most critical behaviors that come up most consistently as barriers, handicaps, and demotivators;

- creating a pool of people who would benefit most from the improvement and getting future-based requests from them, clear *Wows*, suggestions, and ideas;

- generating an action plan, with coaching and support, and activating it;

- following up consistently with the community of people wanting the breakthrough from us;

- measuring, recalibrating, getting better and more nuanced ideas for continuing improvement as we progress.

So, the essence of this approach is to first tap other people's perceptions to get a description of the challenge. Then, we pick the highest yield improvement as a way to drive our own motivation and commitment. With that in hand, we enroll others to support and confront. So, for example, if we most persistently hear the lament that we tend to overemphasize the pluses of courses of action we're excited by and downplay the risks, then we know this would be an area of improvement or evolution that would have both considerable impact on our effectiveness (as perceived by others) and be enthusiastically and supportively received by them.

As we've said before, what gets measured gets done. And so we engage in a course of consistent follow-up, as the way to embed new habits until the benefits of the new habits provide their own natural sustenance and nourishment.

It sounds clear, compelling, and do-able. So, what could the other side possibly object to or offer as an alternative?

Let's see.

It is Not What We Do but How We See and Therefore Who We are Being

While this sounds esoteric, as we'll see, it is as important a perspective, and a surprisingly pragmatic one.

Someone being coached by Omar, let's call him Greg, noticed that one of his co-workers, Larry, was about to march into their common boss's, John office. Greg knew their boss was really incensed by what he considered to be Larry's sarcastic and almost belligerent attitude at a company-sponsored event where external partners were present.

Greg considered intercepting Larry, and giving him a head's up. He also knew their boss was ready to move on and let this go if Larry accepted the feedback. But John had also said within earshot of Greg and a few others that if he got any of Larry's "tap dancing" as he called it, "watch out!"

Greg considered the upside of intervening. He and Larry needed a better working relationship and this would certainly contribute to it. Moreover, Greg had hoped that Larry would reciprocate if he was on thin ice himself sometime in the future.

But Greg stopped himself from acting. Slowing Larry down, getting him to listen, took a lot of energy. Greg felt it was unlikely Larry would acknowledge the help, and would likely say later that he handled it himself without having gained any benefit from Greg's input.

Greg thought of all the times that Larry had not stepped in to help him, how difficult he was, how cantankerous, how flammable, and how he would fervently argue his own perception to the death, often in an immature way.

Well, the anticipated explosion took place. Larry walked into John's office with his usual perceptual blinkers on. John, who had just gotten off a tough call with some partners, wasn't in the mood for Larry's self-justification and lost his cool. He lambasted Larry and told him to manage his attitude, his tongue, his composure, or else... Larry left the office obviously hurt, embarrassed, and angry with humiliation. His eyes briefly met Greg's. Greg tried to quickly rearrange his countenance so it wouldn't appear he was gloating. But Larry looked at him with more than customary belligerence. Did he suspect that Greg knew? Looking stiffly at Greg, he stormed past.

In a later conversation, Greg and Omar analyzed what had happened. We can all probably agree this wasn't Greg's shining moment of leadership. But what list of behaviors could we pinpoint for him to work on? This was a sin of *omission* rather than commission. We can't really catalogue or identify **what doesn't**

happen particularly in non-repetitive situations. When the stance we take towards others is similar to Greg's toward Larry, there are all kinds of things we DON'T do: words we don't speak, actions we don't take, support we don't offer. Here it is what we are NOT that shouts so loudly.

Actually, as so often happens in such situations, Greg in order to deal with his own potential guilt for not acting, mounted an internal defense. He inflated all of Larry's failings and thereby **justified** his own inaction. And if Larry did find out, or correctly intuited that Greg knew and was at least tacitly complicit in what happened, and reacted angrily, Greg would very likely **blame** him for expecting anything else from Greg, given the antagonism and acrimony that Larry had previously (in Greg's description of events) lavished upon him.

By representing himself as a mistreated colleague, and Larry as the diabolical co-worker, Greg is off the hook. In fact, if challenged by Larry, Greg would probably react self-righteously and emphatically.

If we used a behavioral poll, Greg's non-action may not show up as a behavior needing work. The reason: Greg may be just fine habitually in being helpful to those who mesh well with his own tempo, paradigms, or habitual reactions. So what sort of "follow-up" would we do here?

And could we ever get Larry to agree to be among those polled, or Greg to go along with him as being one of his evaluators in a coaching and development process? No way! And we would argue the central problem here is that Greg betrayed his own sense of what he wanted to do. Larry may indeed be immature and a troublemaker. *But Greg still had wanted to help him.* That was his original impulse.

People are never as one-dimensionally bad as we paint them. In fact, we often paint them this way to justify ourselves. Larry (not his real name) is actually a brilliant marketer, who brims with passion and insight, and yes sometimes veers towards being obnoxious and highly impatient.

The problem is that Greg ultimately saw him as an object and a utility—either as a potential resource or irritant. Greg abdicated when he perceived more immediate pain in engaging Larry than the longer-term gain he would have achieved from the relationship-building.

However had Greg also continued to see Larry as a **person**—one not only with faults but also with needs—he would have acted. When we see people AS people, then we sense what they need, what the situation needs, and how we can make our interaction more effective.

"Needs" in this model refers to what is required in order to achieve a common objective.

If organizations are in the business of producing results without killing passion in employees, then we have to see each other as people with abilities to elicit and evoke, and needs to fulfill. That is the only way that we will come to "be" genuinely supportive and therefore "behave" that way too.

The converse is, unfortunately, also true. If we regard someone as an object, we will essentially "be" that way with them, no matter how we behave. For example, we may do all the right things: actively listen, offer help, and even congratulate them. But if done purely as a way to get them on our side or to defuse their resistance, our superficiality will come through. *People will sense we are thinking of ourselves, not them*, even when we claim to be "coaching," "mentoring," or "supporting" them. They may not be able to pinpoint the precise offending behavior, but they will perceive that our fastidiously "acceptable" behavior is a means to an end, either because of the mechanical way we offer help or share information, or even the pro forma way we go through the superficially "positive" motions.

Leaders have to operate "out of the box" as Arbinger would say. In Arbinger's terms, seeing a person as an object is to put him or her "in the box." When we see a person as a person and that's how we relate to them, we are "out of the box" in this sense. Only then will behaviors really matter, or lead to what they should.

Do-Be-Do

Both arguments have valid points to offer. Both also have limitations if not interpreted more expansively. Here's our suggestion for merging them to increase effectiveness and liberate passions.

Whether you are working on your own personal development, or supporting or coaching another, start with "doing." Start with doing where the need is **remedial**—when there is something to fix. Done properly, behavioral change moves us in the direction of being and seeing in a larger way as well.

The reason for this is that two sides of a paradox operate here. One is quite evident. We know we often act the way we feel. Hence, use the Arbinger point of first shifting the way you feel about a person, by shifting how you see them. Our behavior will then evolve naturally and meaningfully.

Then there is the other side of the paradox. William James, the father of clinical psychology, pointed out long ago that we also *feel the way we act*. So if you act a certain way long enough, feelings tend to follow suit. And as the feelings stockpile, a certain "tipping point" in terms of our **being** is achieved. As Alcoholics Anonymous says: "Fake it till you make it." More accurately, "act it until you become it."

For example, Omar coaches several very high-powered leaders who run enterprises or business units worth several billion dollars. These executives do NOT see others as objects, they don't dehumanize people. Yet they still have behavioral challenges.

One is far too Spartan with appreciation and far too lavish with hard-hitting challenges. Another is too cerebral and cross-examines people, rather than engaging them often enough in dialogues of greater creativity or possibility.

Happily, both of them have made substantial progress with these challenges, precisely because they weren't overly defensive once this was objectively pointed out. What helped them avoid the defensiveness snare is their realization that their behavior was undermining the very results they were dedicated to achieving and the very team they were trying to build.

Where it is primarily remedial, go with behaviors. And a good place to start is clearly with the habitual actions that need remedying. Don't expect miracles, but do expect improvement.

Omar's first client will probably never be world-class in sharing appreciation. That's fine. Given his other strengths and his commitment to his people, just some tangible improvement in this area and the evidence of his genuine effort to improve in this regard has gone a long way towards allaying people's anger and recruiting them more fully to help him achieve the landmark results he is known for.

The second client we mentioned has a formidable intellect which will doubtless remain an important part of his arsenal. But he's smart enough to realize that there is more than one communication mode, and when he mellows his relentless rationality, and lets his latent humor and warmth out, people can better hear the sense he's making, and better offer their own ideas too.

On the other hand, when the need is **generative**—when we have to create new options and we are faced with a suite of different situations with no idea which specific behavior will be needed—then work on seeing and thereby being in a more expansive way. So, Greg, who Omar spent some time coaching, in time sought out Larry. He was determined to see him as a person, likely someone who was hurting, humiliated, and who would find it hard to ask for help.

So he decided to make it easy for Larry.

"Larry, I'm really sorry," said Greg. Larry looked up. "For what?" he asked brusquely.

"I could see the boss about to boil over. I should have stopped you and let you know. I'm sorry I didn't."

Larry looked up a bit less testily, with a look of curiosity (we're reporting what was reported to Omar in the aftermath). He was no doubt wondering what was going on.

"Actually," Greg continued, "you and I have had several run-ins, and I just didn't think you'd take me seriously. And if I'm being totally honest, I used that as an excuse not to try. I should have made the effort. Again, I'm sorry."

After a pause, Larry replied: "It's okay Greg. We haven't really made it easy for each other. But John! What a jerk to respond like that!"

Now, Greg had a choice. He didn't really agree with what Larry was saying. Should he jeopardize their fragile armistice? Greg realized however that NOT speaking up would again be to see Larry as an object—as a convenience to manage or manipulate. If he truly related to him as a person he had to try to give him what he needed. And honestly, it seemed that what he needed was another perspective.

Seeking to continue to communicate to a person, and acting out of a genuine concern and desire to help Larry, Greg said:

"Larry I know John blew up. And he shouldn't have perhaps been so extreme. You looked really upset at the event though."

"It was a waste of our time Greg, you must have seen that," Larry said.

"Well, it may have been. But you know whose idea it was? John's. And in front of everybody, our partners and more, one of his top people—you know he trumpets you, and rightly, as one of his top stars—was clearly showing everyone he didn't support the effort."

Larry stopped. He searched Greg's face for any condescension or judgment. He found none. Looking down, he took a deep... breath, let out a mild expletive almost to himself, and then said: "Let me think about that."

Had the earlier, pricklier Greg tried to offer this viewpoint, Larry, feeling he was being evaluated, might have fled from the realization, and counter-attacked, or just denied what Greg was saying. As Greg was truly seeking to provide Larry what he felt was needed, the impression created and the impact were totally different.

Later that day, with some facilitation from Greg who prepared the ground, this led to a dialogue and a chance for Larry to take accountability himself. He was able to apologize to John. John, once pacified to some extent, invited Larry to discuss why he was upset and learned that he felt there should have been more consultation and time to prepare before putting on something so important to which external partners and allies were invited.

Greg had been a powerful change agent. Did he benefit himself? Well his relationships did. The boss saw Greg's facilitation and heard from Larry about Greg's supportive collegiality. More to the point, this team of which he was a part, was currently engaged in several critical projects. As these dialogues cleared the air, the team was able to really come together to retain both purpose and a healthy passion for making progress with those vital projects and advancing their aims, rather than tearing them apart.

Greg's new behavior was credible because it was inspired by a genuine desire to stay "out of the box" with Larry. Yes, some coaching as to possible approaches helped, but only with that backdrop.

Applying This Liberator

So let's do what we can to remedy shortcomings for sure. But then, let's also work on "being" to generate new options with relationships when it's about creating fresh possibilities.

However, thereafter, we have to once more continue to monitor and get feedback on our behaviors (the ultimate custodians of our attitudes) to make sure the new intent is being felt and received as intended. So the prescription is: DO-BE-DO, in other words.

Leadership is a multi-faceted art, requiring a number of practices. Some of the practices emanate from the behaviors we have to remedy or improve, or which others tangibly miss in their interactions with us. Here feedback, application, and ongoing follow-up is the approach *par excellence.*

Other practices however have to do with intuiting what is needed, coming across credibly, and manifesting our deepest and best intent. Here we have to enlarge how we see others.

So these two approaches need each other. "Doing" which is never confirmed ultimately by "being" becomes a mechanistic act of stimulus-response cuckoldry. "Being" that doesn't generate "doing"—particularly doing that is open to "feedforward" from the intended audience—can become delusional and even narcissistic nonsense.

Great leaders will seek for real synergy between these options and seek to express "both/and" not "either/or." As ever, passion *and* performance will be the beneficiaries.

CHAPTER 13

ASK YOURSELF FIRST: CREATING WINNING RELATIONSHIPS

So where does everything we've talked about for the last 12 chapters leave us? Essentially, with the need to create powerful forward momentum for action.

It will be clear that most of the passion liberators we dwelt on are about better, more effective relating. As we said at the outset, almost every corporate pathology, dysfunction, or breakdown can be traced back to inauthentic, dysfunctional, fake, and mediocre relationships.

It is through the quality of how we actively relate to others that we affect the quality of dialogue, idea exchange, mutual stimulus, knowledge sharing, the passing on of learning, and the attempt to create real synergy between talents and potentialities. In fact, how could it be otherwise?

If we consider the act of relating, two key principles help us make some tangible progress. Omar's mentor and collaborator in these areas over many years, M. Scott Peck, outlined in his monumental bestseller *The Road Less Traveled*, the concept of ego boundaries.

Ego boundaries are essentially our understanding of who we are—in other words where we, in terms of our interests and responsibilities, begin and end. Most of us include in this self-concept those we care about (at least to some extent). It could perhaps include some patriotism for our country, maybe some part of our ethnic roots; a key hobby (I am a tennis player, I am a runner, etc), or a part of our identity, neighborhood or town or region (for example in the U.S., Carmel California, West

Texas, Greenwich Village; and in the U.K., County of Yorkshire, the West-end of London, Surrey, among others).

Part of learning to relate and continuing to grow as human beings is to expand our ego boundaries. This means making room for more people, ideas, paradigms, and possibilities in our perception of who we are, in the sense we have of ourselves, and for our understanding of our interests and concerns. The larger the range of our concerns, and the more people and emotions and ideas we can include in our circle of concern, the more expansive we become. Why? Because to open up in this way means to open up our thinking, our capacity to feel and relate, our flexibility, our openness to learning, our "coachability" and more.

So one way to assess the quality of how well we are relating is to see if it *is* opening us up: to new ideas, to a greater range of feelings, to new and progress-affirming habits, and to more collaborative behaviors. If so, our ego boundaries, instead of becoming tauter, will expand.

An organization in which people are growing in self-concept and in the range of ideas and possibilities and in people they can embrace or at least engage with, is going to be a healthier place than its opposite. It will be more alive to possibilities.

In another monumental book, *The Art of Loving*, Erich Fromm points out that when most of us think of love, think the problem is how to find someone to love us; rarely is it about being "lovable" or able to receive love when it is offered.

Or else we think the challenge is how to find the right "object" to love. Almost none of us think we are deficient in the *faculty* of loving.

So most of us might agree relationships are poor. But rarely will we blame our constricted ego boundaries, our prejudices, our emotional immaturity, and our self-absorption—essentially our fear of being transformed. Even more rarely will we blame the paucity of our own attention, or ability to listen or willingness to emotionally engage in courageous, radical conversations.

But truth be told, all the passion liberators are about our *taking responsibility* for expanding our ego boundaries through authenticity, visionary purposes, radical conversations, provoking the future, coaching and more. They are also about improving the quality of our interactions with each other, increasing our faculty of being able to connect with each other, so that we can better harvest our joint potential.

And all this is critical to business success. How? First, as we have said, businesses progress by locating the intersection between what they can best deliver, where their passions are, and where there are substantial profits. And for that "sweet spot," for that epicenter, organizations must state and live into a vision that differentiates them in a meaningful way from everyone else (remember that's the essence of strategy).

Then, organizations need to attract, recruit, induct, coach, inspire, focus and retain the best talent available. And finally, organizations must be able to ensure that the collective potential of the talent assembled is focused on the visionary bull's eye in such a way that the interactions that take place become a net multiplier rather than nullifier of potential and achievement.

Now, we may concede this is truly worth doing. But as leaders sound the call for revitalizing relationships and unleashing latent passion, the first person they have to call out to, to ask, is themselves. *Until leaders ask of themselves first what they are calling for in others, they will have no credibility.*

So leaders must first themselves dive into the passion liberators. They don't have to be perfect at them. They just have to be genuinely grappling with them and be committed to personally progressing with them. In this effort, they would be wise to remember the wisdom of "Do-Be-Do."

As we make the effort though, how will we know we have created the relationships we desire—those that allow us to escape the gravitational pull of laziness, politicking, and evasiveness?

What Success Looks Like

In some ways, the entire book seeks to answer this question. Synthesizing and distilling what we have discussed however, we are left with three non-negotiable demonstrators of potential-fostering and results-delivering relationships:

1. People are authentic, are willing to be known and to get to know each other. They are therefore genuine about their feelings, hopes, fears, ideas, and anxieties.

2. Conversations are brave. They are about what matters. Conversations seek to explore real disagreement, but then mine that disagreement for insight, always seeking to understand the *positive intent* behind each position. Conversations continually seek to bridge to a larger shared future that each party will accept accountability for making real.

3. There is a heady mixture of appreciation and challenge. As we've said, one without the other invalidates the integrity of any sustainable connection between people. And only when we appreciate someone, can we give them the most relevant, apt and credible "wows" or "feedforward" for their evolution as a leader.

We can see the potency of the three if we consider what it is that infuriates people about politicians and political campaigns. As they seek to establish a "relationship" with us, politicians routinely violate each of these three relationship tests.

We almost never get to know politicians authentically. What we have paraded before us are carefully manicured public personas. Handlers and consultants advise them on how to be "likable" and how to assiduously make mainstream and largely uncontroversial statements. However, our intractable problems cannot be solved without controversy. If they could be, they would have been, as the pain they cause is acute.

We almost never are invited therefore to engage in brave, transformational conversations by politicians—those that simultaneously face reality, protect possibility, and provoke a future that we are invited to sacrifice for, commit to, and help make real through our daily choices and actions. We are told what we can receive (though it very often isn't forthcoming once they are in power); few are the politicians who make the transition to being statesmen and therefore ask us to step up to the plate as citizens.

And as for a healthy mixture of appreciation and challenge, we would hope political leaders get that from colleagues, from advisors, from opponents on the other side of the aisle, from reporters, from citizens in open forums. But you have only to read that to have a sinking feeling. Allies are often chosen for their crony appeal; reporters often ask little more than an "acceptable" band of questions; and public appearances most often happen against the backdrop of pre-screened myopically cheering supporters.

We mention this because the cynicism felt towards politicians is something most readers will recognize. We are seeking to demonstrate that this is largely due to their violating these pre-requisites of powerful relationships. Let's make better choices in our organizational and personal lives.

So, we've said, ask yourself first. Most of us would probably buy that as a principle. After all, how can I ask anyone else, if I haven't first asked myself for change and growth and better communication?

But what precisely shall we ask? First, looking at the feedback you typically receive—in particular from the stakeholder coaching community we hope you'll be setting up as we've recommended in Chapter 9—and given the largest challenges in front of your business, or unit, or function, ask "what is the single biggest breakthrough I could commit to, that I would feel passionate about progressing, that will have the greatest impact?"

Assemble a team of internal success coaches. Join their team in the same capacity, and each take aim at the first few personal "bold courageous steps" that would allow you to move past inertia and onto the first milestones of fresh growth. Once you get the momentum going collectively, persevering together will be much easier.

Second, what is it you most wish people in the business would do? Listen more? Connect more to the customer? Speak up? Recognize their people? Bring up the real issues? Challenge the status quo and champion innovation? Whatever it is, discuss it with others, and when you're sure it's the right "first thing," ask yourself first.

Ask your stakeholders: "If I were serious about making a difference in this area, what would let you know I was really making an impact?" And once your boss, colleagues, and team see the effort you're making, if it's the right "first thing," your effort may be *just the thing* to get others joining in. You will at least be part of the "movement" not the "resistance."

Implicit in these first moves is to find and build a community of like-minded constructive renegades; enroll them, bolster them, ideally picking people who are influentials in different quadrants of the organization. Remember it's not instant revolution you're after but consistent evolution.

Finally, model through your own team, what you would like the larger organization to radiate, exhibit, and express. We spoke earlier of Gallup research into high passion/high performance workplaces. Well the cornerstone of their findings was that managers matter more than organizations. In the greatest companies, shoddy leaders devastate morale, exasperate talent, and create a black hole for championship performance. And in the most bleak and beleaguered workplaces, there are pockets of innovation, engagement, excellence, and passion.

Omar has found one, for example, among the Customs and Border Patrol Officers in one of the terminals in JFK. We mention this as these professionals are often considered to be draconian, inflexible, and insensitive. Well, perhaps they can often seem that way. But in one of the terminals, they are a model of service and good humor alongside vigilant professionalism. There is always that choice to make.

If your team can highlight what's possible, and impressive results flow in tandem with the culture you've established, then you've piloted a very compelling prototype. You now have a case to make.

But how do you sustain your own motivation, and why should you make all these Herculean efforts to ignite change, if the larger organization or the senior leaders are too apathetic to lead the charge?

Whenever we've asked remarkable leaders, or read about them—people who've carved out a career, who have managed to hang in there long enough to create a constructive change—their answers have been remarkably similar.

A junior executive who went on to become a key leader in his company was asked why he kept sending up ideas to his company when he got so little feedback... until the day one of his ideas created significant value for the company.

His answer was: "Sure I would have liked to get feedback along the way. But I learned one thing from my father that I never forgot. 'Don't let anyone teach you to be stupid.' I kept coming up with ideas because I get smarter when I think, and life is more fascinating when I'm committed and care."

In short, don't abdicate your quality of life, the trajectory of your career, or the quality of your soul to someone else.

Why care? Because life is more interesting that way.

Why try to do better? Because you'll grow, you'll find ways to make things happen, your skills will get sharpened! That will become YOU and your personal brand.

Many people say: "I'll be motivated if my boss treats me right." Forget it! Don't empower your boss here! Why give your boss control over your motivation, your spirit, and your energy? Why give him control over who you'll be?

If you allow a boss, an environment, to sap your energy, degrade your talent, you will develop dysfunctional habits. Successes and failures have exactly one thing in common... HABITS!

We all say that we're waiting for the "right place" in which to shine. Following the defeatist, stimulus-response philosophy above, the danger is that when we get to the idyllic place, we'll have trained ourselves to be "the wrong person in the right place."

Tom Watson's Secret

Omar saw this played out not too long ago. A leading company that Sensei works with selected a woman as chairman. She was selected over a number of more senior leaders. A number of people asked Omar why he thought she had been selected. He told them that while he couldn't KNOW, he certainly had a hypothesis.

He pointed out that Tom Watson explained how he helped take IBM from being a small company into its almost iconic heyday. He said that he and his team first pictured what IBM would look like as a great company. Next, he said we asked ourselves, "if we were that great company, how would we **behave**?" And then we had to behave that way *today*.

Omar mentioned that this woman leader had personalized this advice. She imagined the ideal role she would like to fulfill in the company. She then asked herself how she would be behaving differently if she already occupied this role. She then challenged herself to behave that way NOW.

So she showed up to board meetings, not just as a marketing director, but with the vision and preparation of a chairman, with the willingness to partner with her colleagues across boundaries, and with ideas on how to add value across the value chain. She thought, felt, and behaved as if she "owned" all of it. Not surprisingly, her current chairman saw this and thought: "Boy, we're really wasting her, she can do so much beyond her current role!"

In any semi-sane company, when we express this, the discrepancy between our potential and our current role will be clear. And most companies will act to capitalize on the increasingly palpable passion and potential they've increasingly glimpsed.

But say they don't. So what? You can't LOSE! All you can possibly do is gain this insight, these perspectives, these skills, and they will add to the luster of your CV. They will allow you to demonstrate how much you were able to achieve even in the lackluster environment you had to work with. And you will develop a real reputation as someone who IS the stimulus, rather than someone perpetually awaiting motivation.

We tend to say, "Give me the job and I'll show you what I can do." That's crazy, every aspirant says that! Rather it should be: "Let me show you what I can do, and if you have an ounce of sense, you'll give me the job." And if you can't give me the job, let's talk about it and see what else we can do. And if you won't, well I'll grow, and I'll have to use the poor leadership I've received as "resistance training" and build my execution and achievement muscles accordingly, and use them for the benefit of another team or organization. Those are all valuable assets to move on with. They are all ways to tap your passion for the real game you're all playing—the game of growth and increasing your capacity to contribute.

And when I AM noticed, and do get recognized, then I have a chance as I move up to positions of greater impact and responsibility, to create the credibility within my company so that I can help it to transform itself.

We all have to learn to *behave our way to our vision:* our vision of ourselves, or vision of our teams; and indeed our dream for the fullest flowering of our company and what it can both be and achieve.

Less lavishly, we have to get good at growing ourselves while helping to "implode" the passion-leeching environments that are desperately waiting for a leader to come along and have them re-invent themselves.

Nothing could be more passion-inducing than to take that on. But just remember, this is not the job for a "lone ranger." It is the job for a member of a talented community, for someone who creates, nurtures, and leverages great relationships. It's just that someone has to kick the ball in play.

Since, as the old saying goes, what goes around comes around, and we will live in the culture we help create—if someone has indeed to start, ask yourself first.

CHAPTER 14

MAKING IT HAPPEN

As we've said, the primary way to deliver any change is to ask yourself to deliver that change first. You need to model the behavior you want others to follow.

Assuming that you do, and also assuming you get your team to follow suit, the question is how can you rescue, rekindle, or liberate passion as an organization-wide undertaking?

There are certain steps you can take. (These steps provide excellent guidance for inaugurating any change since they are anchored in credible relationships.)

A recent book by Matthew Kelly, *The Dream Manager*, makes an important point: people are so disengaged because they cannot see how their work hooks up to their life aspirations, to their dreams.

Kelly recommends as a solution appointing a "dream manager" for each employee. That manager would become a "dream coach" of sorts and help the employee set up and implement plans to realize his/her dreams. Some of those dreams may involve progressing within the current company, some may involve aspirations outside of work, and some may even involve moving on in time.

It's a spiriting fable and essentially a very positive and insightful idea. However, what we're saying, while allied with this premise, is slightly different. We think the danger of having a dream manager by itself is that we will think we can outsource engaging our team. Yes, we partially gain their trust by providing a valuable resource, but we still duck the personal rapport building that has to be the hallmark of building an indigenous performance culture that can evolve *and* endure.

You may or may not want to appoint an internal or external coach to help people take aim at their dreams. But whatever else you attempt, what is inescapable is that all leaders must get to know their team members well enough to understand *at least* two things about them as clearly as possible.

One, what matters to them **today,** not just in the future? What are their current priorities? What gives them joy and satisfaction in the present?

This knowledge is indispensable, as we've suggested before, because our "thank yous," our recognition, our incentives (beyond money anyway) have to track what really matters to the other person.

When incentives are of the type that people most want, whether public acclaim, extra time off, season tickets to a favorite sporting event, inclusion of their family at certain corporate occasions, or help getting a loan, then they will offer us the ultimate expression of their passion: voluntary additional effort and commitment over and above what's needed. This cannot be commanded, as it is beyond what we contractually expect by definition. Rather, it will only be extended when there is inner desire.

But if we don't get to know each other, we won't know the words, the gestures, the type or dosage of appreciation that most gratifies the very people we are seeking to catalyze.

The second thing leaders must come to know is what their people's own vision for their future is, precisely in the sense of the life they dream of leading sometime in the future. Without knowing the largest aspirations of our team members, how will we become their success coaches? How else can we help guide them towards those projects, challenges, or opportunities that will help them create the career or opportunity path they want? And how else will we know when it's right to fight to keep them, or when it's time to get out of their way because we truly can't offer what they most deeply want at this stage of their lives?

But the need to establish this type of rapport and mutual empathy and insight goes even further. As we've hopefully demonstrated, building healthy, open, results- and future-focused relationships will also ensure that people will readily *share passion killers with us as soon as they are glimpsed.* They won't pussyfoot around them, they won't duck the raising of a key issue, and they won't hide bad news for fear of being "shot" like the proverbial Babylonian messenger.

So, if you decide to kick off an initiative whereby liberating passion becomes a mainstay, start with building relationships among the senior team and let it ripple out from there.

But what if, in addition to our successively deepening relationships spiraling out throughout the organization and adding value on their own terms, you want to make liberating passion and liberating peak performance along with it, a major corporate initiative? Can it be done?

We keep hearing that people have "initiative fatigue." This is nonsense. No one decries new things. They complain of "lack of completion" fatigue. They object to only being inundated with the bureaucracy of new initiatives and rarely to experiencing the associated courageous decisions, future-creating actions, and promised results.

Often once the sizzle fades, all that's left is the bitter taste of pointless meetings, exhortations, and busy-work. Nothing new has happened.

On other hand, when we really commit to personally taking on the change ourselves visibly and emphatically, people will respond with all due excitement to initiatives. What's new, as long as it's REAL, relevant, and productive, will then naturally engender productive enthusiasm.

Creating Real Change

The five cardinal sins of misleading change efforts are:

1. **Too much hype. Not enough action.** Many change efforts begin with a major internal PR campaign that often eerily resembles a National Political Convention complete with pomp, ceremony, a big kick-off meeting with rousing speeches, lots of photo ops, and evocative music. All of these accompaniments can be powerful as long as they garnish, instead of substituting substance. One client came to Sensei for help after the company's overproduced "rock concert-like" change effort elicited nothing more than

company-wide cynicism and a tab of millions of dollars. *Let's hype the actions we're actually taking*, not just our intentions and plans.

2. **Over-advertise how "massive" the change will be, and only deliver iterative tweaking.** One company we worked with terrified everyone in the organization by telling them that the upcoming change in their way of working would revolutionize everything. Structures would change, policies would transform, and a value-based evaluation of all elements would occur. But after being jolted awake by the loud, pompous blast, people subsequently found their energy and belief in the undertaking fizzling. They saw the same things happening as always, with perhaps a few incremental shifts. As a result, they shut down mentally and dug into their old status quo bunkers with even greater zeal. Not surprisingly, this well-known brand name ended up being merged with another company.

3. **Create a frenzy and then just spend all your time in committees and meetings.** After hyping all that needs to happen, after trumpeting the true magnitude of the changes and transformations, people who have been whipped into a frenzy now expect not only action, but decisiveness, speed, and urgency. Instead, they encounter endless meetings, Power Point slide shows and committee debates on the wording of various banners. Confusion rises and frustration flourishes as these committees invariably create training sessions and busy work that build up the appearance of action, but neglect all the really challenging aspects. Unfortunately, part of the reason often is that such committees have neither been empowered nor held accountable. *Let's create instead some fast-action teams that represent a cross-section of the organization, make them accountable, and ask them to deliver.* And let's have them demonstrate the value and relevance of every recommendation, course, and initiative as being required to deliver the touted and advertised change.

4. **Make no changes in senior leadership.** The old way of working, the one we're now deriding and lampooning, was

created by our current leaders. Hence, either they have to demonstrate how they will change, or else a number of them will have to be replaced by people who are clear exemplars of the new way of working and interacting. The client mentioned above, who came to Sensei too late for a rescue operation, had a highly controlling and inflexible chief executive who kept heralding the need for change and decentralization. The overwhelming feedback we gathered about him was: "It's like Woody Allen telling you to get over your neuroses, or Winston Churchill telling you cigars are bad for you." (When younger leaders responded to the verbal gauntlet he threw down by taking on the responsibility that was being asked of them, he stopped them in their tracks for daring to step out of bounds. A few such encounters and all the speeches in the world are dead in the water.)

Let's admit that past failures of leadership have created some of what we're facing, and then let's clearly make sure we aren't perpetuating more of the same.

5. **Involve no customers, ignore the market.** The change we're igniting lives or dies by producing market value. Hence customers are a marvelous sanity check. If we can involve them in our design, in our brainstorming, in our idea generation, and in our assessment of leaders, we'll have a remarkable impact. Sensei worked with a Johnson & Johnson operation on a vision challenge. After articulating a compelling vision, with Sensei's help they brought in their suppliers, business partners, some distributors, and major customers. These outside people, coupled with J&J team members, looked at the current reality and the gap between it and the vision. "How well are we living this vision today?" was the question posed. Invariably, customers and suppliers saw the success of the implementation of the vision very differently from the corporate cheerleaders. By the time the session concluded, they had received both wonderful affirmation on some fronts (what they were already doing very well), and a bracing manifesto for improvement on the other. Having now gone public with external stakeholders, it was far easier to get going and to drive the priorities. *External engagements help keep our ideas fresh, urgent, and exciting. This*

will in turn initiate and sustain meaningful action. If relationships are the key to passion and performance, it shouldn't be surprising that building richer, more interactive partnerships with clients and suppliers as well will pay rich dividends both materially and otherwise, and be a powerful inducement for our change effort to succeed.

The fundamental challenge of change therefore is that it ultimately depends, as does all leadership, on our passion and on the relationships and communication that foster or flummox it. Whether aiming for an operational breakthrough or for the re-invention of the company, remember that it is the depth and breadth of the relationships that are fostered and the quality of the conversations that take place that finally predict our success or failure.

It has been noted: "Nothing can be built that is larger than the relationships on which it is based." And if the relationships don't transform and evolve, the rest of the process certainly won't. If you detect that the quality of listening and interaction is not consistent with the sweep or magnitude of the expressed change agenda, then solving *that* problem has to be the first priority.

What to Do

For organization-wide change of any type to succeed, all leaders must:

- Share a leadership vision and overall values in common. Bridges can be built across other differences, but rarely over this one.

- Believe that they can personally help lead and deliver what they are asking of others.

- Understand that their daily priorities and behavior have to underwrite and validate the change.

- Be coachable and open to feedback, as a way of modeling that requirement for others.

- Achieve personal satisfaction from achieving this goal *together* with their colleagues and teams.

So let's not tilt at windmills. Let's pick the change and growth challenges necessary to liberate passion and vitalize our key relationships and make sure we meet those challenges in concert. Let's leave the PT Barnum-type antics to hucksters. Real leaders helping to produce real value for potentially outstanding teams have to go for change selectively, constructively, personally, and, above all, credibly. The *passion of their example* and the *sizzle of the actions* have to be where the real ad campaign emanates.

Let's Engage

We produce results together, by and large. If instead of fighting the need to communicate and grow beyond our comfort zones, and we can make our peace with these needs and indeed welcome them, then virtually anything is possible. Passion will then continue to burn bright.

Nathaniel Branden said it so evocatively: "This earth is the distant star that we must somehow find a way to reach." We must reach each other in other words—that's the only way forward.

As a leader, we have to know that people will agree to focus productively and follow our lead with zeal and vitality when four things are true.

One, they are inspired and excited by at least the common goals, ideally by our visionary purpose.

Two, they believe our personal commitment to it is genuine and that we will create a believable game plan on that basis.

Three, they care about the people they are going to deliver it with.

And finally, they are convinced that it will be good for them as well.

For all of us in any and all roles, when we have made peace with the fact that we can all only grow, develop, and deliver *in relationship* with each other, then passion will flow towards making a difference. And ultimately, where passion flows, our future goes with it.

We will therefore not fear bringing all of who we are to work. And all of us will be welcomed as long as we welcome the fullness of our colleagues; as long as this shared acceptance leaves room for constructive yet appreciative challenge; as long as we are signing up to partner and collaborate and co-create a future we all are committed to.

So, let's start to create the kind of relationships and therefore the kind of future we want. Let's behave in a way that taps and amplifies the best of our passionate purpose and commitment. *Let's behave our way to our vision.*

Why would we settle for anything less?

INDEX